A PHYSICAL APPROACH
TO PLAYING THE TRUMPET

Lynn K. Asper
First Edition

WaveSong Press

Hudsonville, Michigan

WaveSong Press

1138 Fairfield Dr.
Hudsonville, MI 49426
(616) 457-0562

Library of Congress Catalog Card Number: 98-94064

ISBN 0-9668847-0-1

Printed in the United States of America

This book is dedicated to my mother, Doris,
who claims she never had to make me practice.
I know better.

TABLE OF CONTENTS

TABLE OF FIGURES

APPENDICES

A Method Book Based Upon Physical Techniques

Why a physical approach? There are numerous other trumpet playing techniques which, when properly applied, work well for some players. Other teachers believe that a physical approach is not necessary because, they contend, the body will learn the proper way to play if the student listens long enough to a desired trumpet sound. Still other teachers, usually fine players themselves who may never have needed to work through physical barriers, demonstrate by playing for their students. I call this the "watch me and do it like I do" approach.

My physical approach attempts to avoid intangible concepts by explaining the physical skill to be applied to each area of playing so that the student can learn the *correct physical response* for every playing situation. Tangible, concrete, logical. This method can be taught in a step-by-step manner and students find that it is a very understandable way to learn.

A Physical Approach to Playing the Trumpet is based partly upon my belief that a body or a body part that is not responding properly is unable to correct itself through listening to more literature or "playing through the problem" until the situation changes. My experience tells me that the body will likely *not* correct itself and I have seen too many students practice incorrect habits waiting for a day that will never arrive!

A Physical Approach to Playing the Trumpet is a proactive way to identify barriers to playing improvement and apply specific techniques to overcome those barriers. It is based upon the science of how the body works, making it possible for the student to see and feel changes as they occur. The student has immediate feedback and does not lose precious time which might have been devoted to practicing bad habits.

Why Write a Book?

I have probably written this book over 200 times! Throughout my years of teaching I have found that I do a lot of writing for each individual student in order to explain the physical approach. I've grown a bit concerned that I might not be saying the same things consistently among students - especially when I have several new students at once. I've realized that I could save myself a lot of time during lessons, ensure consistency, and, hopefully, clarify my philosophy if I just collected my ideas and wrote them down one last time in a book. I have already discovered, based upon a draft version of this book, that my students are better able to understand the physical approach concepts if they have them in book form that they can read and re-read. Lastly, I truly believe that I have important information to share with trumpet players. This could be anything from overcoming a basic playing barrier for the less advanced player to increased technical proficiency for advanced players.

How This Book is Organized

This book was written for intermediate and advanced trumpet students of all ages and their teachers. You will notice that the book is written in a first person, question-and-answer format. Throughout my years of teaching, I have found that I can anticipate many of the questions that students tend to ask about the physical approach. Since I have personally answered these questions hundreds of times before, writing in this conversational format simply seemed natural to me. It also makes the book useful to persons who wish to improve their trumpet playing without the assistance of a teacher.

When this book is being used by a teacher with a student, the teacher becomes a trumpet playing analyst. Over time and with practice, the student should become better and better at analyzing their own playing, so that barriers can be overcome through the use of this book and the techniques described even when a teacher is not immediately available.

The first section of the book is devoted to defining the technical aspects of the physical approach. Figures and photographs are used to reinforce the written descriptions. However, knowing *how* to practice is as important as knowing *what* to practice. For this purpose, daily warm up, frequency of practice sessions, and endurance-building topics are also covered.

Specific musical examples are located in the Appendices at the end of the book. Various units throughout the book will address how to use these exercises. Grouping the musical exercises together at the end of the book will eventually make them easier to locate and practice. Once the student understands the intent of each exercise, they will not need to flip back and forth through the book to find an exercise.

In my many years as an educator, I have discovered that each of my students has also had something to teach me. This connection has been very important to me and I realize that teaching through a book does not allow for this type of interaction. I would welcome your communication at lasper@post.grcc.cc.mi.us or (616) 234-3941. My address is Grand Rapids Community College, 143 Bostwick NE, Grand Rapids, MI, 49503.

ABOUT THE AUTHOR

Lynn K. Asper is a native of South Bend, Indiana, holding a Bachelor of Science in Music Education from Ball State University and a Master of Music Education from Michigan State University. With a father, Franklin Asper, who played trumpet under the baton of John Philip Sousa and a trumpet-playing older brother, Norman Asper (whom Lynn still considers to be his first teacher), it was just destiny that Lynn would become a trumpet player and teacher.

Robert Ralston, Lynn's beginning band teacher in South Bend, was also his first official trumpet teacher. By the ninth grade, Lynn was studying with Jay Miller (ret.), a graduate of Indiana University. During his undergraduate years at Ball State University he studied with Max Woodbury, who was at that time a member of the Indianapolis Symphony Orchestra, and Boyd Hood, who was the trumpet instructor at Ball State University. Lynn considers Boyd Hood to have had the greatest impact upon his trumpet playing. Mr. Hood had studied with Adolf "Bud" Herseth, principal trumpet with the Chicago Symphony Orchestra. In graduate school at Michigan State University, Lynn studied with Byron Autry (ret.).

Lynn K. Asper spent ten years teaching high school music at Ottawa Hills High School in Grand Rapids, Michigan. He was asked to join the music faculty at Grand Rapids Community College in 1979 and has remained there in the capacity of Music Department Head, conductor of the Kent Philharmonia Orchestra, Director of Instrumental Music, professor of trumpet, and conductor of numerous college ensembles, including the GRCC Wind Ensemble, Raider Marching Band, and the Community College Orchestra.

ACKNOWLEDGEMENTS

I would like to acknowledge the following people who helped make this book a reality:

- All the trumpet students who have passed through Grand Rapids Community College;
- Greg Wells, our model trumpet player in the photos and trumpet major at Grand Rapids Community College;
- Lyons-Russell Photography, Grand Rapids, Michigan;
- My wife, Renée, who lovingly pushed me until this project was finally finished;
- Wayne Rosebury, George MacKeller, Dan Duncan, Glenn Jarrell, Edie Dunnette, and Kevin Dobreff who helped me edit drafts;
- My son, Ben, for his technical advice regarding anatomy and physiology;
- My son, Bret, for his business management consultation;
- Dr. I. Edward Alcamo, Ph.D. and Random House, Inc. for the use of the muscle drawings originally produced for Anatomy Coloring Workbook;
- Marcia Van Horn, for her talent in designing the covers, technical assistance, and willingness to share her knowledge of the publishing industry.

What are reflexes, and how are they used in trumpet playing?

reflex \'re-fleks\ n. 1. An automatic and often inborn response to a stimulus that involves a nerve impulse passing inward from a receptor to a nerve center and thence outward to an effector (muscle or gland) without reaching the level of consciousness - called also reflex act; compare habit

One way to interpret this definition is to see reflexes as only those inborn physical actions over which we have no control. An example of this type of interpretation would be the pupils of your eyes dilating when the lights dim or your leg moving when the doctor taps your knee with a small mallet. In a broader sense, we can think of reflexes as physical actions learned over time and by repetition that become so automatic that you no longer have to think about them to make them happen - any more than you think about your pupils! What if those automatic reflexes could be applied to trumpet playing...?

When we were small children, at some time we learned about *hot*. Our parents said, "Don't you touch that, it's hot!". Well, we touched it anyway, and it *was* hot, and we got burned. The next time our parents said, "Don't touch that, it's hot!", we thought about it for a minute, we *still* touched it, and we got burned again. After several encounters with outdoor grills, electric heaters, stoves etc., we not only learned to listen to our parents, but our bodies learned something as well. Our sense of touch identified extreme heat in a split second and sent a signal to the brain to pull the hand away from the heat. This learned and now automatic response is called a *reflex*. We no longer go through the thought processes to react to extreme heat - our body has learned to automatically respond correctly. Reflexes like the one in this example save us from harm, save us time, and free up the conscious part of the brain to concentrate on other activities.

How are these reflexes built and maintained?

Our bodies build and maintain hundreds and hundreds of different reflexes through repetition. For many of the musical reflexes, we initially have to use conscious thought to know how to respond. After the reflex is developed, our conscious thoughts are available to deal with other activities such as sight-reading, counting, or following the conductor. For the musician to develop all of the necessary reflexes required to be successful, repetition must be specific and frequent - it's called *practice*. (You didn't really think that this method was so amazing you wouldn't have to practice?)

Is repetition of a reflex always a good thing?

Students sometimes feel as if their playing skills have leveled off or reached a plateau. These are students who, through no fault of their own, have developed bad physical playing habits - reflexes, which they unknowingly reinforce every day by their constant use. In this case, repetition of a reflex *can* be a bad thing. If the reflex you learned wasn't good to begin with, practicing it won't make it better!

How are reflexes triggered?

One way to trigger a reflex is by conscious thought. I have students use this method in the beginning when learning each reflex. Once the proper reflex is practiced by repetition, less and less conscious thought is required.

Most of the time reflexes are triggered by our senses. I suppose that all senses could come into play when playing the trumpet, but the ones we use mostly are sight, hearing, and, to a certain extent, touch.

Do reflexes ever decay?

Absolutely! If reflexes are not continually and properly reinforced, they *will* decay. If they are reinforced improperly, they will build improperly. We will refer to correct practice as *conscious thought reflex-building* or *conscious thought practice*. We will use conscious thought reflex-building as part of the warm up every day.

How many trumpet playing reflexes are there?

I have identified eight trumpet playing reflexes. They are listed separately here for convenience and ease of learning. Actually, all eight are interrelated and learning one reflex often depends upon learning another reflex. Development and application of each reflex listed will be described in detail in the upcoming units.

1.   Body Carriage (position of the head, arms/shoulders, legs/feet, and hands)
2.   Embouchure
3.   Air Intake
4.   Tongue Strike
5.   Tongue Height
6.   Anchor
7.   Pivot
8.   Air Column

Does the concept of "mind over matter" come into play here?

Now, I don't want you to think I've gone over the edge, but in a way, yes. If we could train our senses to produce the correct reflex perfectly every time our senses sent information to the brain, we could play correctly and musically anything that was put in front of us, *every time.*

Is this possible?

I have heard players come very close to perfection. We all have. But we are human and even well built reflexes will decay if not continually reinforced. Reality dictates that there is no such thing as perfection. However, we should always *strive* for perfection, knowing that it may never be achieved. I believe that if we practice proper reflex-building in an orderly and organized way, we have a better shot at improving our trumpet playing than if we leave it to chance. I believe that a physical developmental approach is extremely efficient, especially for we humans. We learn so many other behaviors via reflex-building, trumpet skills can be seen as just another set of learned skills. A complex set of skills, certainly, but related to other learning. With this organized yet natural approach, we are not asking our bodies to do something magical or mystically inspired. You don't have to be born with "the gift" or inherit some intangible talent. You can teach your body to play the trumpet!

So, what do I need to do?

We need to make sure that your practice routine has structure and goals and continually works to help the mind learn to react correctly to incoming sensory information. Then the mind must respond by sending correct signals to the body for appropriate muscle responses. The muscles must be well developed and strong enough to be able to respond to the incoming signals.

UNIT 2   THE BODY CARRIAGE

How you position certain parts of your body is the first set of reflexes we will discuss. Having to learn how to sit, stand, and hold the instrument may seem odd, since we sit and stand every day of our lives. However, correct body carriage for playing the trumpet is *not* necessarily something that occurs naturally. So we start by learning the **body carriage** reflexes. The **body carriage** reflexes are a set of related reflexes from various body areas that contain major muscle groups, such as the legs, arms, shoulders, etc. Because our body operates as a unified whole in order to play the trumpet, we learn the correct position for each of these areas and bring them together.

What is the correct position for my head?

The head should be held straight up as if it were on a pole, perpendicular to the floor when seated or standing. This position will allow the throat, or trachea, to stay open without any bends or constrictions. Do not allow the head to tilt forward or backward.

Figure 1

Position of the Head

What is the correct position for my arms and shoulders?

The upper arms should hang freely in the shoulder socket with the shoulders very relaxed and free from tension. The trapezius muscles of the shoulder are the most likely to have too much tension. This is most often caused by raising them. Work to keep the trapezius muscles relaxed.

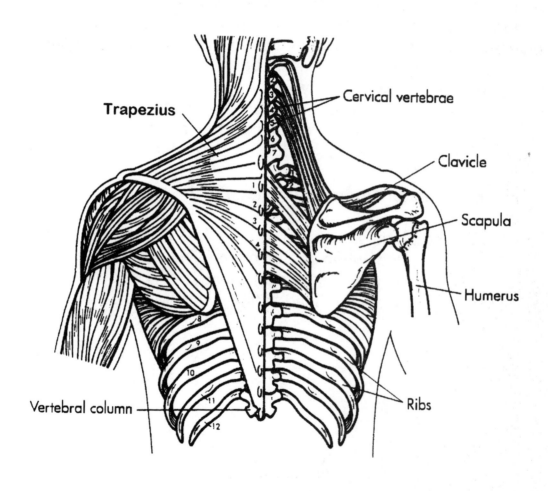

Figure 2   Muscles of the Shoulder - Trapezius

What about my legs and feet?

This position will obviously be different when you are seated or standing. While seated you have two choices. For students with short legs, you should sit with your feet flat on the floor with your seat toward the front of the chair. This position will keep your back straight, your spine vertical over your hips, your head erect and your throat, or trachea, open. Students with long legs should sit with your seat in the back of the chair, with your feet under the chair. Remember what is important here: *keep your back straight, your spine vertical over your hips, your head erect, and your throat open.*

Figure 3

Seated Position

If you are standing, the back, spine, head and throat positions are easier to maintain since your hips are already under your spine. To feel more stable while standing, put your feet about shoulder width apart. This will allow for good balance and the ability to move around a bit without falling down. The "feet together" position used by some marching bands is not very good for proper balance. Be careful not to keep reinforcing this old improper reflex.

Figure 4

Standing Position

What is the proper hand position?

Our goal here is to hold the trumpet with as little tension as possible. The trumpet should actually be held more with the left hand than the right, and I prefer to think of *hanging* the horn on the left hand rather than *holding* it. This also promotes a more relaxed left hand position. All the fingers of the left hand should wrap around the third valve casing with the ring finger used for manipulating the third valve slide. The left thumb should go around the first valve casing. *Do not grab the trumpet, simply let the horn hang on your left hand. Relax!*

Figure 5   Left Hand Position

The right hand must be relaxed for ease of finger flexibility. The right hand fingers must be curved so the tips of the fingers can push the valves straight down. The trumpet may be tilted *slightly* to the player's right to help with alignment of the fingers and the valves.

You should visualize having a tennis ball in the right hand, then curl the right thumb underneath the ball. Move the right hand to the trumpet so the first three fingertips line up with the three valves, and place the right thumb under the leadpipe. If you have small hands, place the tip of the right thumb under the leadpipe between the 1st and 2nd valves. If you have large hands, place the tip of the right thumb under the leadpipe between the 2nd and 3rd valves. *Keep the pinky finger out of the hook/ring.* The pinky finger in the hook/ring is used only when holding the trumpet while turning pages with the left hand.

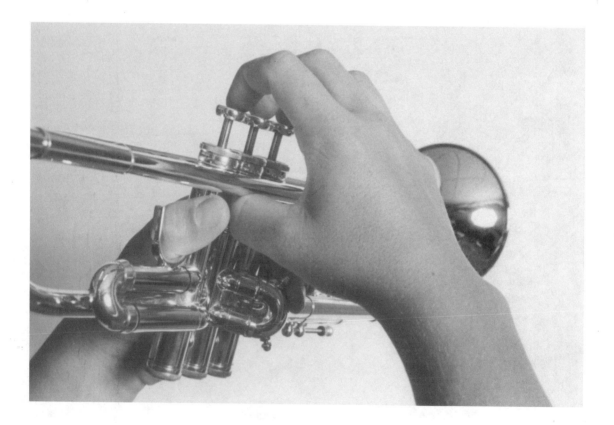

Figure 6 Right Hand Position

The key to proper trumpet hand position is a combination of alignment and relaxation. Proper body alignment will help assure correct air flow through the throat. Too much tension in either hand will promote pulling the trumpet toward the face. Too much pressure from the trumpet on the face will cause fatigue very quickly.

What is the air column and how is it used to play the trumpet?

Air column is the process of gathering air into the body and properly using it to play the trumpet. It is the next reflex we need to understand and begin reinforcing. It is easiest to grasp this concept by following along with the experiment described below.

Let's do an experiment. Visualize two tubes. The tubes are identical except for the fact that one is larger in diameter. At one end of each tube there are identical air compressors, and at the opposite end of each tube there are identical air-speed indicators.

Question: If each air compressor can push identical amounts of air at identical speeds, *through which tube will the air move faster?*

Answer: The tube with the smaller diameter.

Now let's suspend an identical piece of material in each tube, and blow air against them.

Question: Will the pieces of material vibrate?

Answer: Yes, when the air goes fast enough.

Question: When the pieces of identical vibrating material vibrate, will they each produce a pitch?

Answer: Yes.

Question: When the pieces of vibrating material in each tube have identical volumes of air flowing against them (creating a pitch), will the pitches be the same?

Answer:　No, the piece of vibrating material in the smaller tube will vibrate at a higher pitch than the piece in the larger tube.

Let's suspend another piece of vibrating material in each tube. Now each tube has two pieces of material vibrating inside it.

Question:　The first piece of vibrating material we put in each tube was rather thin. The second piece of vibrating material we put in each tube was rather thick. As we send air through each tube, will the two pieces of vibrating material vibrate at the same pitch?

Answer:　No. The thin piece of material will vibrate at a higher pitch than the thick one.

The two pieces of material, although vibrating independently, contribute to an overall sound produced in the tube. Let's say that the sound produced can be measured upon a scale from "dark, warm, open and wide" to "bright, cold, closed and narrow".

Question:　If we could control which piece of vibrating material contributes more to the sound, and we chose the thin piece, where on our "dark versus bright" scale would the resulting sound be located?

Answer:　The sound would be more on the "bright, cold, closed and narrow" end of the scale.

Question:　If we could get the thick piece of vibrating material to contribute more to the sound, then where on the scale would the resultant sound be located?

Answer:　The sound would be more on the "warm, dark, open and wide" end of the scale.

What does this experiment have to do with trumpet playing?

Our lungs and abdominal muscles are the air compressor, our throat, or trachea, is the tube, the upper lip is the thin piece of vibrating material, and the lower lip is the thick piece of vibrating material.

How do I vary the diameter of the tube?

There are two ways to do this. The first way is to raise and lower the tongue in the mouth by forming the vowel shapes: "oh", "ah", "eh", "ih", and "ee". Moving from one vowel shape to another will change the speed of the air *as it passes through the mouth,* without changing the size of the air tube, or trachea.

Note: Faster Air = Higher Pitch

The second way to vary the diameter of the tube is by closing the throat, or trachea. I will refer to the trachea as the throat for the remainder of this book. Although medically incorrect, I believe it is easier to understand for our purposes. I do not recommend the throat closing technique until the player is quite advanced. Once the throat closes, for any reason, it tends not to open back up all of the way. We must almost always play with an open throat to use our air efficiently.

What happens when I just blow harder, doesn't that speed up the air?

Yes, it does to a certain extent. However, blowing more air also produces a louder sound. Many young players discover this, and never learn any other method for playing in the upper register. This is mostly why many trumpet players can only play in the upper register at a loud volume. If the music calls for a high note at a soft volume, the player who uses this technique is stuck.

I know that I need to take a big breath to play the trumpet, but how do I know if I'm taking in enough air?

Many students do not know what a big breath feels like. Your body may never have experienced a full, deep breath and has no frame of reference. We all *think* we can take in a big breath when we, for example, try to blow up an inflatable toy.

So let's try another experiment. Go to the local hardware store and buy yourself a ¾" plumber's connecting tube. It will cost about $.30. The plumber's connecting tube is made of plastic and is used to attach two pieces of pipe internally. Be sure it is ¾" and not ½". The ¾" tube is just about the size of the opening around the trumpet mouthpiece.

Clean the tube well, then place about half of the tube in your mouth, sealing your lips around it. Put your tongue in the bottom of your mouth like you're saying "ho", and breathe in. *That's what a deep breath feels like.* If this feeling is new to you, you should do this exercise several times at the beginning of your practice session. Your body will, over time, learn to recognize this as the feeling it should experience when a deep breath is required. After a while, you'll only need to use the "plumber's tube" occasionally for reinforcement.

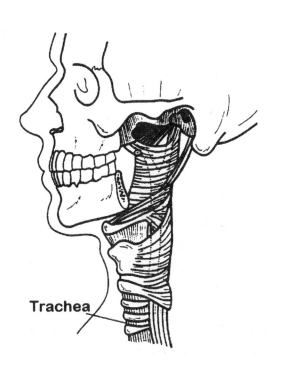

Trachea

Figure 7

The Trachea

UNIT 5   THE EMBOUCHURE

What is the proper embouchure?

em·bou·chure \am-bu-shu(e)r\ n. 1: the position and use of the lips in producing a musical tone on a wind instrument

Consistent with the other reflexes we have studied so far, the proper **embouchure** is as efficient as possible. As you can see from Figure 8, there is a muscle called the orbicularis oris which is in the shape of a ring surrounding the opening of the mouth. This muscle forms the support for the **embouchure**. The strength of this muscle is directly related to endurance and flexibility to play in all ranges. Developing this muscle through disciplined practice will increase the amount that can be placed under the mouthpiece ring, which increases the amount of vibrations that can be achieved. Play on muscle!

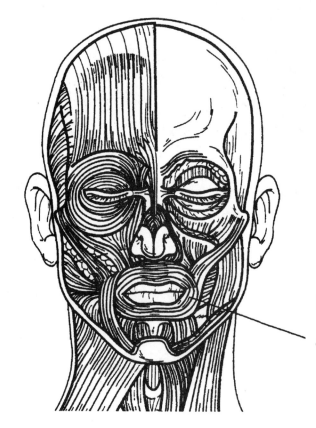

Figure 8   Muscles of the Face

Orbicularis Oris

When forming the trumpet **embouchure**, the lips should be rolled in slightly while being held firm at the corners. The mouthpiece must be placed on the lips so as to allow as much upper lip to vibrate *inside the mouthpiece* as possible. This lip formation should closely resemble the shape of the orbicularis oris muscle structure and should be held firmly for most playing. When the trumpet player experiences fatigue, it should be in the area of this muscle structure, *not the flesh where the mouthpiece contacts the face.*

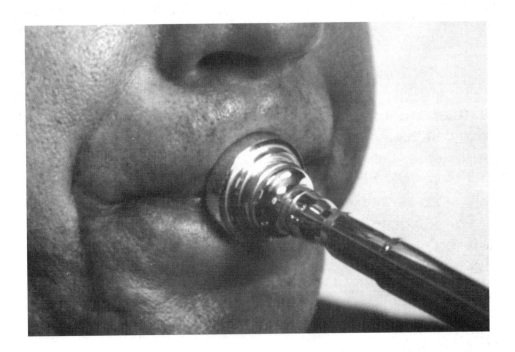

Figure 9   Mouthpiece Placement

When I put the mouthpiece on the embouchure, how much pressure should I use?

There is no such thing as "no pressure", but you should use just enough pressure to seal the mouthpiece to the lips so there can be no leakage of air around the mouthpiece. We must be wary of using too much pressure because it can cause premature fatigue.

Should the weight of the horn be the same on each lip?

Most of the time you will play with most of the weight of the horn on the lower lip. We will alter this slightly when playing in the pedal range.

How will I alter this?

In order to understand the relationship of mouthpiece placement to playing in various ranges we need to define three key reflexes: **anchor, buzz,** and **pivot.**

Even though we would like to use only as much pressure as is necessary for a good seal, the weight of the horn has to be someplace. We need to determine where to place the mouthpiece in order to maximize lip vibration. For example, if we want to play a mid-range to high note, we want to have as much upper lip vibration as possible. We would put the weight of the horn on the bottom lip. The actual placement of the weight of the horn on the lips is a reflex called the **anchor.** If we need to play a low to pedal-range note, the bottom lip could help us by vibrating a little more, so we could put some weight on the upper lip. If we needed to play a note in the middle register, the weight of the horn would be equal on both lips, or stay on the bottom lip. We'll actually move the **anchor** from one lip to the other while we are going from the upper register to the lower, or vise versa. This horn weight movement is called the **pivot.** Notice that I have intentionally used the word "weight" not "pressure".

How are the anchor and the buzz related?

The **buzz** reflex is actually the sound that the lips make inside the mouthpiece cup. They make this sound *vibrating separately*. Although the lips come close to each other inside the mouthpiece, they are independent vibrators.

There have been some recent laboratory experiments which indicate that the upper lip does most of the vibrating during the **buzz**, and that the lower lip only vibrates sympathetically. Most of the time, trumpet players are called upon to play in the middle to upper register of their instrument. This means that much of the time the **anchor** will be placed on the bottom lip allowing the upper lip to do the vibrating. I believe that, although the lower lip doesn't vibrate nearly as much as the upper lip does in the **buzz**, placement of the **anchor** slightly on the upper lip will allow the lower lip to vibrate sufficiently to open up the lower register of the trumpet, especially in the pedal range. This will make the sound warmer and darker.

How does the pivot affect both the buzz and the anchor?

Actually it's the **buzz** that is affected by the other two. Remember, the **pivot** is the movement of the **anchor** from the bottom lip to the top, such as would be necessary to play an arpeggio starting on a low note. Having the **anchor** placed on the bottom lip most of the time will allow the top lip to vibrate more freely. When the top lip vibrates freely, the tone quality becomes wider and more open. When the upper lip is pinned down by mouthpiece weight, especially when playing in the middle to upper register, the resulting tone quality will be pinched, thin and narrow.

When learning the **pivot** initially, you will move the horn substantially. As your body understands what the **pivot** reflex is, the movement will become a subtle combination of horn, jaw, and **embouchure** movement.

Figure 10   Horn Pivot for Mid to Upper Register

Figure 11   Horn Pivot for Low to Pedal Register

Notice that in Figure 11 the lower jaw has swung out to meet the bottom of the mouthpiece. This is due to the fact that the jaw is hinged, and will need to be protruded to compensate for the fact that the bottom of the mouthpiece has been pulled slightly away from the face. This technique, along with further discussion of the pedal range, will be addressed in detail in Unit 15, Daily Warm Up Exercises.

UNIT 6   AIR INTAKE

In Unit 4, **Air Column**, we discussed the movement of air, the speed of air and it's relationship to pitch, and what it really feels like to take a big breath. This unit will help you apply these concepts by teaching you the next reflex, **air intake.**

Now that I know what a deep breath feels like, should I always breathe this way?

Yes. We should always take a full, deep breath. This process is referred to as **air intake.** The amount of air we take in should not be affected by length of phrase, dynamic level marked, or any other factor. *Take in maximum air all the time!* When taking air in, you must form the vowel "ho" and breathe in just as you did with the plumber's tube in your mouth (Unit 4). I call this taking a "ho" breath and even have a special breath mark I use when marking literature - " ○ ".

One last point about **air intake,** or full, deep breathing. For some reason, we tend to take air in during the one beat prior to our next entrance. If the tempo is 80 beats per minute or faster, this does not allow us enough time to take a full, deep breath. I would prefer that you take *one full second to breathe,* no matter how fast the music is marked. This may seem awkward at first and takes lots of practice.

If I take a full, deep breath all the time, won't I almost always have more air than I need?

Yes, but this is a *good* thing. How many times have you been told to "play with breath support", or "you need to support your sound". Did anyone ever tell you what breath support really is? Breath support is *air in reserve*. This can best be achieved by striving to perfect your **air intake** reflex so that it is consistent.

Might I spend as much time exhaling as I do inhaling?   Yes.

I understand what buzz is, but what is buzz pitch?

Buzz pitch is the actual pitch made by the buzz, or lip vibration, inside the mouthpiece cup. This pitch controls the quality of the sound made on the trumpet. Phrases such as "that horn has a big sound" are misleading and generally not true. Horn design has some effect on the sound, but it is the trumpet player's technique that has more effect upon the breadth and depth of the sound they can produce. The smallest horn *can* produce a big open sound - just as a large horn *can* produce a narrow, pinched sound. It is true, however, that some horns are built so that the big open sound is easier to achieve. The key to remember is that *breadth and depth of the trumpet sound is directly related to the pitch of the buzz inside the mouthpiece cup - the lower the buzz pitch, the wider the sound.*

Buzz pitch can be controlled two ways. The first is by contracting and relaxing the lips as they vibrate inside the mouthpiece cup. The second is by moving both the teeth and the lips together - essentially a biting motion. I recommend that you use only the first method. In the second method, the biting action results in thinning out the tone, and it is much more difficult to control than the first method. Experimentation with the first method described will allow you to control the width of the contractions and learn the point at which too wide is out of tune. This control will come with practice.

Is the buzz pitch something that can be practiced?

I was never much of a "practice the buzz" person until I realized how much effect it had on my playing. I am still *not* an advocate of practicing the buzz without the horn or mouthpiece. However, I have become a believer in *mouthpiece buzzing* every day. Unit 15, Daily Warm Up Exercises, will provide more detail about how to practice the buzz pitch. However, let me say here that daily mouthpiece buzzing will give you control over buzz pitch by isolating the reflexes that control the contraction/relaxation of the lips.

What tonguing technique should I use?

In talking to friends and reading trumpet technique books in preparation for writing this book, I have found that I teach tonguing differently than most trumpet teachers. In the Preface I referred to the impact that my first trumpet teacher, Bob Ralston, had on my playing. Bob is a fine french horn player and he taught this tonguing technique to me. I suspect that the differences in how I teach tonguing may have to do with this exposure to french horn technique. I have found french horn players who tongue this way. However, I have not found many trumpet players who tongue the way I do. Generally speaking, the goal of tonguing is to produce sound with a clean, clear attack with no fuzzy or airy sound prior to the pitch. This must be possible at all speeds and dynamic levels. Here is how I approach tonguing with my students.

In order for trumpet tone to be produced, the lips inside the cup of the mouthpiece need to buzz. We can get the lips to start buzzing by simply blowing air into the mouthpiece/horn until the air speed is sufficient to start the lips buzzing, thus producing a sound. The sound, however, will be delayed because it takes some time for the air speed to get to a sufficient velocity to start the buzz. We need a little puff of air to help us create that air speed *immediately*. This is why we tongue.

Be wary of a tonguing technique which calls for the tongue to do "it's job" by touching the back of the upper teeth where the roof of the mouth meets the back of the upper front teeth, as if you were saying the word "to" or "tea". The puff of air created by this technique then needs to drop down approximately ¼", and go between the teeth in order to get the buzz started. When I hear a student with a fuzzy and airy sound on the beginning of a note, I know what I'm hearing *is the actual sound of that puff of air dropping down and moving between the teeth.* One way to eliminate this airy attack is to tongue harder, creating a heavier puff. This is not a pleasant sound and it is not a technique I recommend.

What if you could create that puff of air closer to the lips? That would eliminate the need for the puff of air to have to travel to the lips to initiate the buzz, nor would it require the player to use a heavier tongue. To achieve this, the tongue should come between the teeth and actually touch the top lip right below the top teeth. This tongue placement is part of the **tongue strike** reflex. The top lip is curled in slightly and pulled in against the top teeth making this technique very easy to use. Instead of the hard "to" and "tea" sounds, you should use the consonant and vowel sounds; "tho", "thah", "theh", "thih" and "thee". The different vowel sounds relate to tongue height which relates to air speed and pitch. One caution! *Do not put the tongue between the teeth too early.* This causes a heavy, thudding sound I call "pulling the plug". Timing is everything!

This **tongue strike** tonguing technique allows you to tongue more cleanly and eliminates the airy front on the note. It can be done with tremendous single tongue speed and can easily be applied to multiple tonguing after the single tonguing technique is learned. This technique also facilitates both staccato and legato tonguing styles because it allows for the buzz to be interrupted at precisely the point you desire. The buzz will then restart as the tongue is pulled away. This air stream, or buzz, interruption completes the **tongue strike** reflex. Note that the word *strike* is not used in the context of harshness or hitting, but as in a "snake" strike. The recoiling of the tongue is immediate and efficient, as in the strike of a snake.

In Figure 12, page 27, the horizontal line is the air stream and the vertical line is the **tongue strike.** You can see that the tongue interrupts the air stream, or buzz, without stopping it. The resultant sound is then legato - connected and smooth. Since the legato tonguing technique is dependent upon an air stream which is interrupted but not stopped, the legato tonguing style will be learned prior to the marcato style - disconnected and separated. The **tongue strike** is a critical reflex to learn and will require time and effort.

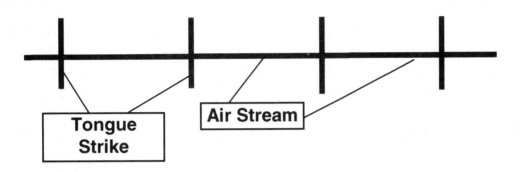

Direction of Air

Figure 12   Tongue Strike Graphic

UNIT 9 THE SOUND PRODUCTION CYCLE

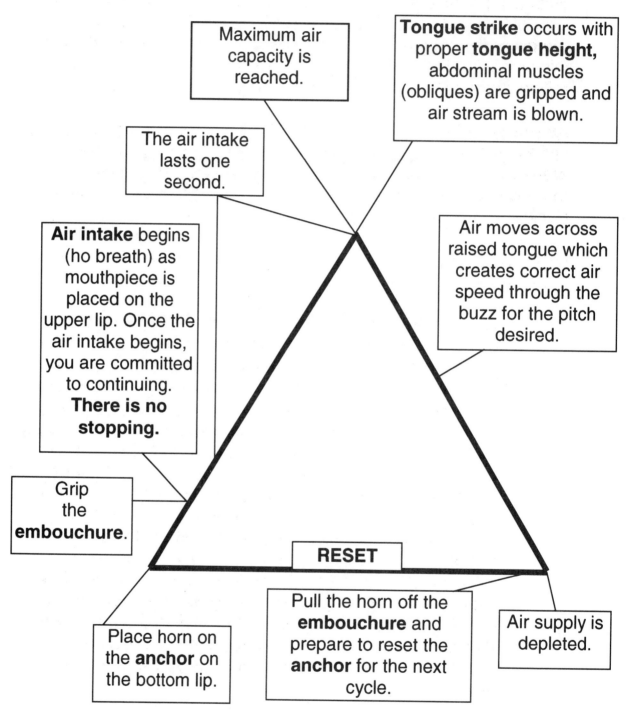

Maximum air capacity is reached.

Tongue strike occurs with proper **tongue height,** abdominal muscles (obliques) are gripped and air stream is blown.

The air intake lasts one second.

Air intake begins (ho breath) as mouthpiece is placed on the upper lip. Once the air intake begins, you are committed to continuing. **There is no stopping.**

Air moves across raised tongue which creates correct air speed through the buzz for the pitch desired.

Grip the **embouchure**.

RESET

Place horn on the **anchor** on the bottom lip.

Pull the horn off the **embouchure** and prepare to reset the **anchor** for the next cycle.

Air supply is depleted.

Figure 13 The Sound Production Cycle

What is the Sound Production Cycle?

The Sound Production Cycle is the *progression of interrelated reflexes* which must take place as we position the trumpet on the embouchure, take air in, set the embouchure muscles, tongue, and blow air. As you see in Figure 13, page 28, I use a triangle to represent this process. I've seen similar graphic representations of this process using circles, but prefer the triangle because specific reflexes occur at the corners of the triangle.

As you can see from Figure 13, the Sound Production Cycle may be divided into separate areas, each represented by a box in the drawing. Although all trumpet playing reflexes are important to build, the reflexes pertaining to the set-up section of the Sound Production Cycle are the most important.

Let's look carefully at each section of the Sound Production Cycle from Figure 13:

- We start at the bottom left hand corner of the triangle by setting the **anchor.** As stated earlier, much of the trumpet player's time will be spent playing in the middle to upper register. For the sake of discussion, let's define this range as treble clef 1st line Eb to the top of the horn - wherever that is. For most players, this will constitute approximately 2/3 of the playable range of the trumpet. The other 1/3, below 1st line Eb and extending downward to F# below middle C, will be extended by practice in the pedal range. For this reason we should set the horn on the bottom lip first since it is the lip which vibrates the least. Set the horn where it feels comfortable for you, making sure that the bottom of the mouthpiece is placed on the orbicularis oris muscle, which supports the bottom lip. This placement should be done so that the mouthpiece is in the middle of the lips and muscle structure. Most experienced players will find that they already place the mouthpiece correctly and very few will have to change this placement.

- Next the **embouchure** is gripped so that the muscle structure resembles the oval shape of the orbicularis oris muscle itself. Great care should be taken here to concentrate on tightening the embouchure at the corners, which will in turn firm up the rest of the muscle. As this gripping occurs, each lip should be firmed and rolled inward slightly so that much of the red part of the lip actually disappears underneath itself. The lips always remain on top of the teeth - never roll them under the teeth.

- As the **air intake** begins, you are committed to continuing through to the end of the note or phrase. Do not stop for any reason. The tongue should be dropped to the bottom of the mouth so that the sound of "ho" can be heard as the air is taken in through the mouth. At this time the mouthpiece should be placed on the upper lip. It is important to note that the actions of gripping the **embouchure**, taking the "ho" breath, and placing the mouthpiece on the upper lip occur so that they are *nearly simultaneous*. Proper upper lip placement is most crucial. The word "place" should be emphasized. Many students get into trouble at this point by placing the mouthpiece on the upper lip and pinning the upper lip down with the weight of the horn. This stretches the upper lip because the tendency is to then pull part of the lip back out of the mouthpiece in order to play. This action will thin the lip and cause it to fatigue faster than the rest of the **embouchure**. This improper reflex must be unlearned and eliminated. Instead, without using much pressure, place the mouthpiece on the upper lip with as much muscle as possible under the mouthpiece ring, and with as much lip as you can place inside the mouthpiece. *Once the mouthpiece is placed, don't move it.* This can be the hardest thing for most trumpet players to learn. However, through repetition this will become natural and unconscious.

- As mentioned earlier, many wind players tend to breathe in during one beat of the piece of music being played, normally occurring during the last beat of rest. Unless the work has a metronomic marking of 60 bpm or less, the time allowed for the **air intake** is not long enough to ensure that a proper full, deep breath will be taken. For this reason, the breath should always occur for at least one second.

- When maximum air capacity occurs, indicated at the top of the triangle, the **tongue strike** will occur. The height of the tongue will be controlled by the pitch desired ("tho" for the lower register, progressing through "thah", "theh", "thih" and "thee" for the upper register). Since the tongue will come through the teeth slightly touching the upper lip, the force behind the tongue will be quite light. The internal oblique muscles of the lower abdomen are then gripped, and the blowing of the air begins (see Figure 14, page 32).

- As the air is blown, the lower abdominal muscles (obliques) continue to contract as the air is expelled.

- When the air is depleted, indicated by the bottom right hand corner of the triangle, the horn should be removed from the **embouchure**. The horn is then reset on the **anchor.**

Practicing the Sound Production Cycle is done every day during the warm up. When the cycle is actually applied to music, the player will take another breath at the bottom right corner of the triangle and continue without removing the horn from the **embouchure**. The triangle in it's entirety is actually only used when practicing long tones. Reinforcing these reflexes during the warm up every day will allow you the opportunity to use conscious thought practice and isolate each reflex that needs focused practice.

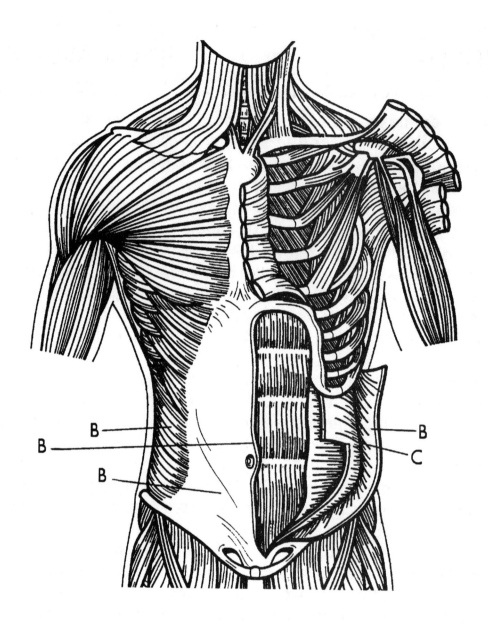

Figure 14   Muscles of the Lower Abdomen - Obliques ("C" and "B" in the above drawing)

What needs to be warmed up each day and why?

Playing an instrument is a physical endeavor. Many would say playing a brass instrument is almost athletic in nature. An athlete would never just start doing an athletic activity without first putting the body and mind through some kind of routine which prepares oneself for the physical activity. *You are an athlete* and you should prepare yourself each day for the activity of trumpet playing. The warm up will be applied to both the mind and body.

All of the trumpet playing muscles in the body need to be warmed up. This includes the muscles of the face, neck, shoulders, arms, hands, abdomen, back, and legs. These are all areas of the body, which are crucial to playing the trumpet. The muscles of the face, hands, and arms must actually be used in a systematic manner to become ready for today's trumpet playing. The remaining muscle groups mentioned above must at least be *analyzed* for their preparedness for playing the trumpet today.

Why do the muscle groups need to be analyzed each day?

Remember, reflexes will decay if they are not properly reinforced on a consistent, daily basis. The mind is responsible for sending the correct signal to the muscles for the music to be played. It is also responsible for analyzing the results of the practice you do. Therefore, it is very important to warm up *mentally*. This type of activity occurs during the daily warm up and is called "conscious reflex practice". As you proceed through the daily warm up exercises later in the book, you will learn which reflexes need to be analyzed, and in which part of the warm up this analysis occurs for each reflex. For this reason, the warm up exercises are quite lengthy and specific. Too many students spend too little time warming up the body and the mind, and do no analysis of their playing during that time. As a consequence, bad reflexes continue to be built and reinforced.

This lack of attention to the daily warm up is probably the single most important factor contributing to becoming stuck on a "skill plateau" in trumpet playing. When students come to me and say they feel like they're not getting any better, it is usually related to the fact that they have not identified any trumpet playing reflexes, consequently, they don't work on reflex development every day. This can result in a short and unfocused warm up. They lack the tools needed to solve their trumpet playing problems.

There are eight trumpet playing reflexes (the **body carriage** reflexes are combined) which must fire correctly to play well. Since the signal sent from the sense receptor to the brain and back to the muscle is *electrical* in nature, I use the term "firing" in reference to reflexes. It is very difficult to practice all eight of these reflexes at once. I have found, over the years, that the brain can only concentrate on three reflexes at any one time. It may be possible to address four at a time if the fourth reflex contains one of the **body carriage** reflexes since these large muscle reflexes also seem to be the easiest to learn. Reflexes must be *isolated* so they may be reinforced and analyzed individually and in small groups during the warm up.

The ability to *isolate* reflexes is the first of the two factors which determine the length and complexity of the warm up.

How often do I need to warm up?

The warm up must be done every day. If, for some reason, you are not playing or practicing on a particular day you should still warm up. The reflexes need to be reinforced daily.

How many parts does the warm up contain, and how much time should be spent on each part?

The warm up contains four parts:

Part I	Mouthpiece Buzzing -	3 - 4 minutes
Part II	Long Tones -	8 - 12 minutes
Part III	Descending Slurred Arpeggios -	6 - 8 minutes
Part IV	Ascending Tongued Arpeggios -	8 - 11 minutes
	Total	25 - 35 minutes

Why is there so much time flexibility?

Your readiness to play the trumpet will vary from day to day, and is controlled by many factors such as the amount of playing done on the previous day, what your playing demands are for today, your mental preparedness, and your physical preparedness. The warm up routines at the end of this book will address specific situations such as warming up on the "morning before" or the "morning after" a performance. These instances will require a warm up of a different length and are affected by their proximity to a rehearsal or performance. Even when you do not have an upcoming performance or rehearsal, each day may require that you spend more time on one section of the warm up routine and less time on another. It's not unheard of to have days in which it takes 45-50 minutes to warm up. The process of warming up must be tailored to your needs and will change from day to day.

How does rest affect the warm up?

Rest is the second factor which determines the length and complexity of the warm up.

After muscles have rested overnight, they must be reacquainted with their trumpet playing role slowly and deliberately on the following day or there may be risk of abuse. The key to pacing during the warm up routine is to *rest exactly the same length of time that you play!* I have

A Physical Approach to Playing the Trumpet

found that this is singularly important. Too many students rush through the warm up without regard for the consequences.

Which reflexes do I reinforce during the warm up?

Part	Description	Reflexes Reinforced
One	Mouthpiece Buzzing	Air Intake Embouchure One Tongue Strike Air Column
Two	Long Tones	**All reflexes from Part One and...** Body Carriage Tongue Height - Single Note Anchor
Three	Descending Slurred Arpeggios	**All reflexes from Parts One and Two and...** Pivot Tongue Height - to pedal register
Four	Ascending Tongued Arpeggios	**All reflexes from above and...** Four Tongue Strikes Tongue Height - to upper register

As you can see, reflexes are cumulative as you move from one part to the next. Each of the previous reflexes is expected to continue to fire correctly after you add the new ones to the routine. Reflexes *firing correctly, without conscious thought,* is the real goal in trumpet playing. The warm up session gives us the opportunity to analyze how this building process is progressing, how it's working today, and exactly which reflexes are giving us the most trouble.

How does the warm up affect the rest of my practice session?

The results of your warm up session directly determine what and how you will practice for the day. If your warm up goes fairly well and you have identified a couple of reflexes that are inconsistent that day, then you may continue practicing but with *special conscious thought* given to those reflexes which are not firing correctly or consistently.

On the other hand, if your warm up goes poorly and it seems that almost no reflex is firing correctly, do not continue practicing in the normal manner. You should go directly to the prescribed exercises for each reflex, which are outlined in the back of this book. If you disregard your analysis and continue to practice in the normal manner, you will continue to reinforce bad reflexes!

What if I have a rehearsal?

If you are warming up prior to a rehearsal and the warm up is going poorly, be extremely careful. I would pick out one or two reflexes that need more attention and spend the entire rehearsal concentrating solely on them.

How will I feel after the warm up is completed?

If you have warmed up properly, you should feel as if you haven't done any playing at all. Since you have rested as much as you have played, you should not feel tired. If you feel tired, you have warmed up too fast.

UNIT 11   THE LESSON

What is the role of the trumpet teacher during my lessons?

Each trumpet teacher will approach the lesson somewhat differently. When the theories set forth in this book are utilized, the teacher acts as your trumpet playing analyst. I do that by listening to the student's playing, analyzing what I hear in relation to all of the reflexes which need to fire, suggesting which reflexes need attention, and assigning a practice routine to accomplish the reflex-building which needs to take place.

Who teaches the teacher?

I personally teach myself. Each day I analyze my playing during the warm up to make sure most things are working properly. If I hear something that needs attention, I do the exercises needed for reflex reinforcement, and then I go about my practice routine. If I encounter a problem that I can't seem to fix, I seek advice from another area professional trumpet player.

How do I analyze my own playing during practice sessions and rehearsals?

One of our main goals is for you to become your own trumpet playing analyst. Most of the analysis you will do comes on a daily basis *during the warm up* period. This is the time when you are consciously evaluating how your body is working that day. As the warm up progresses, you will make determinations about whether reflexes are firing well enough to continue your practice routine, or whether you should spend most of your session working only on reflex-building. The musical examples and exercises for building each reflex are contained in the Appendixes.

Analysis during rehearsals is more difficult. You will have discovered during your daily warm up whether you are having a good reflex day or not. If the answer is no, you will need to pick the reflexes which need the most attention and concentrate on those during the rehearsal. If the whole rehearsal goes poorly, you'll probably need to spend some time later that day or the next doing reflex-building. The biggest problem with rehearsals is that you have to concentrate on making music with other musicians, listening, reacting, following the conductor, etc. It is very difficult to think about or change individual reflexes during this busy time, however, this is another technique that can be acquired through practice. What your body usually does is use old reflexes to do the job for that rehearsal. This reliance upon old, improper, inefficient reflexes will reinforce them, thus creating the need to tear them down later and rebuild the correct, more efficient reflexes.

Once I've made the analysis of my playing, what do I do with the information?

If reflexes are firing well during the warm up period, you will continue your practice routine. If the analysis identifies reflexes that need to be reinforced prior to continuing, you will have a set of exercises to work on for each reflex. There will be a specific time set aside each day for reflex-building and maintenance practice. There will also be specific time for other kinds of practice. If you need much work on reflex-building, other practice routines will be skipped for awhile. Unit 12, Practicing, will detail how to deal with this situation.

What should I be practicing on a daily basis?

Your daily practice should be divided into four sections: the warm up, literature, technical studies and exercises. Note that many times the terms "technical studies" and "exercises" are used interchangeably. The term "exercises" will be used here to describe specific exercises used for reflex-building. Technical studies will denote technical practice not specifically spent reflex-building. All of these practice components will probably become part of your lesson with your teacher. Once the warm up process is clearly understood, you should arrive at the lesson already warmed up.

UNIT 12   PRACTICING

How often should I practice?

I suggest that you practice two times per day with each session lasting approximately an hour. This routine should be followed six days per week. It is acceptable to take a day off from practicing each week, but you will *warm up* every day whether you practice or not.

What should each practice session contain?

Daily Practice Session 1

- Warm Up - 25-35 minutes

    Buzzing
    Long Tones
    Descending Slurred Arpeggios
    Ascending Tongued Arpeggios

- Literature Practice - 25 minutes

    Solo Literature

Daily Practice Session 2

- Technical Studies Practice - 25 minutes

- Reflex-Building Exercises - 25 minutes
      or
- Endurance Practice - until fatigued

Is the order of practice important?

Yes! Some students tell me that they are not morning people, but everyone is revived and fresher after a night's rest. After a proper warm up, I prefer to have students practice literature when they are fresh physically and mentally. Spend this time making music! Unless you experience significant problems with reflex firing, try to forget them while you practice literature and see how they work under performance conditions. Take stock of what reflexes you might need to address later this afternoon or evening during the second practice session of the day, just don't do it now unless your playing is so poor that improvement cannot be made.

I like to end each practice day - session two, with either reflex-building or practicing for endurance. This type of practice can be accomplished even when you're a little tired. Literature is difficult to practice when tired, so address that during session number one. Separate the two practice sessions by at least two hours. This will allow for some recovery of the **embouchure** muscles.

What do I do if I can't play a musical figure?

You must reduce the figure to the smallest element that can be practiced. Then try to decide whether the problem is related to rhythm, speed, intervals (leaps), or finger dexterity. I will give you hints about how to address these problem areas, and which reflexes will help you solve each problem.

What if I can't play a figure up to the speed indicated?

Every student should own a metronome, and should use it during the practice session each day. I prefer the digital type metronome that is capable of clicking the sub division of each beat such as the Seiko DM - 20, but any good metronome will do.

If you cannot play a figure up to tempo (tempo can be defined as beats per minute, or bpm), use your metronome to do the following:

1. Slow the figure or musical section down to the tempo (bpm) at which you can play it perfectly 12 times, and document that number.
2. Write the goal tempo down, and subtract the tempo at which you can currently play it perfectly.
3. The resultant number will then need to be divided by three.
4. This will give you the number of days it will take you to reach your goal.

Example:

1. I can play the section perfectly 12 times at 80 bpm.
2. The music says I need to play this at 120 bpm.
3. If I subtract 80 from 120, the resultant number is 40.
4. 40 divided by three is 13.33 or 14 days.

OK, but how do I use metronome practice?

The idea here is to practice speed in small pieces, and also to have success each day. Many students play a figure a couple of times, have some success, then try to go faster and faster, eventually reaching a speed beyond their reach. Then they end their practice on this figure in a negative frame of mind. If you knew ahead of time that you could reach your goal in small steps in 14 days, each day you could speed up a number of beats per minute that is small enough to feel insignificant. Today I can play the figure at 80 bpm. Tomorrow my goal is 83 bpm. Is the difference per day significant? *NO!* But will 3 bpm times 14 days be significant? *VERY!*

When the metronome is set only 3 bpm faster each day, the brain doesn't even sense the difference. Each day a small goal is attained. Each day you are successful. This success-oriented frame of mind is vital when learning new skills and facing new challenges on a daily basis.

What is "back-chaining?"

Another effective method for practicing technically difficult passages is referred to as "back-chaining". This is the process of separating a musical passage into small parts, such as measures or beats, and learning the *last part first.* Once that part is mastered at a selected speed, the measure or beat just prior to the last part is learned and the two are played together. This process of moving backward through a difficult passage is repeated until the entire passage is learned. When music is learned in this fashion, the student becomes proficient throughout the entire passage rather than mastering the beginning section at the expense of the later parts.

If I get tired when I play, how can I build up my endurance?

Endurance practice must be part of your weekly practice routine. Most of the time you should allow two full days between endurance practice sessions. This pace would have you doing endurance practice twice per week. You should do the endurance practice at the end of a practice day and should not have any performances within the next week. Endurance practice will be covered in greater detail in Unit 19, Practicing for Endurance.

UNIT 13   METHOD BOOKS AND LITERATURE

What method books do you recommend and how will they be applied to my practice routine?

Although there are numerous fine method books on the market, I recommend purchase of the following:

- 100 Studies for Trumpet, by Ernst Sachse
- Technical Studies, by Herbert Clark

As a trumpet player and teacher, I continue to use these books at least every other day. You will probably find that you will use these books for the remainder of your trumpet playing career.

How will these books be used?

As you recall, the second practice session each day is devoted to practicing technical studies and exercises. Technical studies and exercises selected from these books will concentrate on the building and maintaining of certain reflexes.

These two books are only two of hundreds of books that could be used. I use these particular books for specific reasons. Many students have difficulty with musical passages in certain keys. Many times this difficulty can be traced directly to the fact that little practice is done in every key, and difficult fingering patterns are rarely practiced with any consistency. For finger flexibility in all keys I recommend the Clark book.

Articulation problems are quite common and usually require significant practice. These problems are usually traced to inconsistent tonguing reflexes. Although the Sachse book has many other uses, I use it to teach students to place the tongue in the correct position for speed in scale-wise and intervalic motion. The Sachse book sets up a progression of difficulty which builds speed and accuracy of the single tongue.

What solo literature do you recommend for advanced high school players or collegiate players?

The Recommended Literature List, Appendix G, will give you an idea of the variety of literature that can be studied. There are, however, two standard works that should definitely become part of your repertoire. Performance of the Haydn Concerto for Trumpet and the Hummell Concerto for Trumpet is expected of the collegiate player during the first two years.

Do I need to learn scales?

Yes! I recommend that you learn all major and minor scales in every key. Scales are the musical language used to create all other musical works. Players must become conversant in all major and minor scales in all keys in order to be truly proficient in any type of music. Scale study does serve a purpose.

UNIT 14   BUYING A TRUMPET AND MOUTHPIECE

How do I pick the right trumpet?

This is a very complicated question, but I will share my thoughts on the subject and my approach to finding the right horn for you.

If you are a trumpet major or already play professionally, you should be playing on a professional model trumpet. Many companies have produced what they call "intermediate level" trumpets. In my opinion, these instruments are nothing more than stripped down versions of the professional instrument. If you have an "intermediate level" or a "starter" instrument and plan to move up and acquire another horn, go to the professional model. Remember, you do not have to buy a new instrument. A good used instrument with all the correct qualities may suit you well and save you some money in the process.

At the undergraduate level I prefer to see students purchase one horn which can be effective playing all types of music. It could have a *tendency* toward a certain type or style but it is not a good idea at the undergraduate level to purchase an instrument that has only one use. For instance, many jazz players prefer a light weight, bright instrument which has a lot of edge and is capable of producing high levels of volume. These players will want a medium-large instrument with a bell and leadpipe set-up that produces this sound. On the other hand, orchestral and band players prefer a slightly darker sound and would lean toward an instrument slightly heavier which will produce the darker sound. These players will tend toward the large bore horns. This can be very confusing, so I'll tell you my approach.

Pick an instrument which tends toward the kind of playing you will do *most of the time.* Some adjustments for sound variety can be achieved through mouthpiece selection. Next, find a retail store where you can sit for a couple of hours and just play horns. There are also catalog companies that will send you horns on consignment. Start by playing

46

horns produced by different manufacturers. One company's instruments will start to feel the best to you. When you consider a manufacturer, stick with the big four: Bach, Benge, Shilke and Yamaha. Once you have picked the manufacturer, then play different models of horns. Play several models with different bore sizes and leadpipe combinations; medium-large bores, large bores, heavy, light, gold plated, silver plated - until you find the one that you like best. Don't listen to your friends or be swayed by glossy promotional material when deciding which one to buy. Choose the instrument that you think makes you sound your best. This decision is yours and yours alone. You should spend no more than $1,100 to $1,300 for a new instrument, or $500 to $750 for a good, used professional trumpet.

There are several companies that build custom handmade trumpets for a lot of money. I would not consider these horns until after completion of your undergraduate work, and after deciding to make your entire living playing the trumpet. Then you may feel comfortable spending this amount of money!

How do I pick the right mouthpiece?

This is another very complicated question, but here is my opinion.

Too many trumpet players believe that the bigger the mouthpiece the better you are as a player. This is a myth! There are several guidelines that should be followed when picking a mouthpiece.

The part of the mouthpiece that rests against your lips is the ring. You should try to play on the largest ring you can handle. "What you can handle" is determined by the amount of playing, in hours, that you do each day. Ring sizes are indicated by numbers. Nearly all companies use "1" to indicate their largest ring. A 1 ring, for example, is a mouthpiece for players who play four to five hours per day. Some undergraduates play that much - many do not. A number 3 ring is commonly used by musicians who play two to three hours per day, and is the size that fits most players' embouchures. Be honest with yourself about how much time you actually play each day when selecting a ring size.

After you have established the ring size that fits you, you may then vary the cup depth to help change the quality of the sound. The cup is the rounded part of the mouthpiece and it's size is indicated by letters. For most manufacturers, an "E" cup is the shallowest and an "A" cup or a cup with no letter at all is the deepest. Cup depth, in addition to affecting the quality of the sound, also affects the ease with which high or low registers will respond. For example, the higher register will respond better with a shallow cup, however, tone quality may suffer to achieve this.

My recommendation is that all advanced high school and collegiate players should play a mouthpiece that has a standard #27 throat. The throat is the hole at the bottom of the cup and it's diameter is indicated numerically. The lower the number, the larger the mouthpiece throat.

The throat of the mouthpiece is the top of the backbore, which is the inside of the tapered section of the mouthpiece that goes into the trumpet itself. By varying the amount of taper of the backbore, we can affect the amount of air that can be put into the trumpet. This is experienced as resistance. The amount of backbore taper is indicated numerically. Varying the amount of backbore taper will vary the degree of resistance.

Warburton Music Products specializes in the manufacture of mouthpieces for brass instruments. Warburton's mouthpieces come in component pieces that include various sized rings, cups, and backbores. These individual component pieces then screw together to form a truly customized mouthpiece for each player's individual needs. The player, through a process of trial and elimination, finds the mouthpiece configuration which matches the type of playing they do. Usually, the player finds one certain ring size that they use on all the mouthpieces they own. Then, through the use of different sized cups and backbores, they can have specialized mouthpieces for various types of playing.

Does this mean that I may use more than one mouthpiece?

Yes! You may, for example, use a mouthpiece with a specific cup and backbore for jazz or marching band use. You might then use a different cup and backbore for playing in a band, wind ensemble, or orchestra. Both mouthpieces would utilize the same ring.

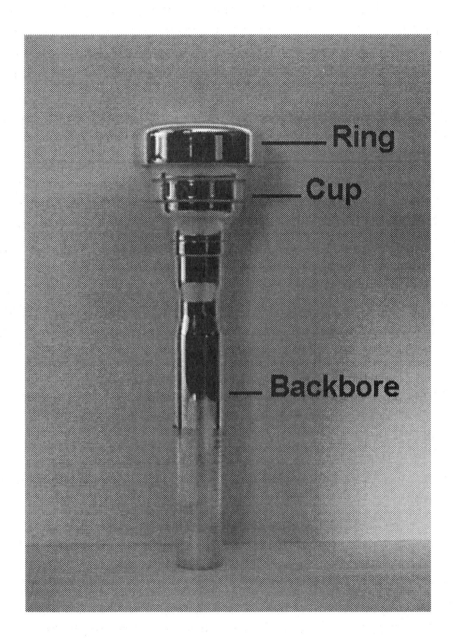

Figure 15   The Mouthpiece

UNIT 15   DAILY WARM UP EXERCISES

Daily Warm Up

Your daily warm up will consist of four parts: mouthpiece buzzing, long tones, descending slurred arpeggios, and ascending tongued arpeggios. Even as you are practicing the musical exercises in Part I, Mouthpiece Buzzing, you will also be attending to what *type* of warm up you should be doing that day, e.g. normal, morning after, short, etc. For example, you may know that you have a major performance tomorrow, so today you will do the "morning before" warm up. Generally speaking, the first part of this warm up will still be mouthpiece buzzing, the second part will be long tones, etc. This unit is divided into the four basic parts of the *normal* daily warm up. Then additional detail is provided to help you apply warm up concepts to special circumstances such as "morning before".

Before you begin:

- Unless you have memorized the Sound Production Cycle from Unit 9, it may be a good idea to review that graphic carefully at this point.
- One warm up session lasts the entire day - even though you have two practice sessions.

Part I - Mouthpiece Buzzing

Normal Warm Up

The normal warm up is used on days when nothing unusual occurred on the previous day. In this circumstance you should start with Appendix A, Daily Warm Up Exercises, Part I - Mouthpiece Buzzing. Use this exercise in the following manner:

- Eventually you should start on a low F#. If that is not possible at this point, you should start on as low a note as is possible for you.
- If you are not sure what note you actually started on, you will make an attempt to figure it out later.
- Try to start on a lower note each day until you can start on the low F#.
- Make a mark on the page where you start and stop. *Document your progress.*
- Buzz the rhythm at the tempo marked and always *rest as long as you played* when you get to the fermata over the rest. It is extremely important that you allow your muscles to recover after each two-measure exercise.
- Slurring from note to note is done by lip contraction only. This will build strength and control over the buzz pitch.
- You are isolating four reflexes in Part I Mouthpiece Buzzing:

    Air Intake
    Embouchure
    Tongue Strike
    Air Column

- Concentrate on the four reflexes and analyze today's response:

    Air Intake should be full and relaxed. Use the one-second breath.
    Embouchure is gripped as **air intake** begins.
    Tongue Strike occurs as the tongue lightly touches the top lip through the teeth as in saying "thu", producing immediate tone.
    Air Column should move through the buzz producing a wide, fat tone.

- Progress through the exercises, resting as marked, until you reach the point where you feel your throat starting to close to control the air. At this point, *STOP!*
- Tomorrow, try to do two things:

1. start the exercise on a lower note
2. go higher before the throat closes

- Continue expanding the range of Part I each day until you can complete the entire exercise.

If, at this point in the warm up, things are going very poorly, do not continue to Appendix A, Part II yet. You should, instead, do the Morning After Warm Up, spending more time on the single note long tone buzz on the mouthpiece. In this case, you should concentrate on the first four reflexes for the entire practice session, completing only Parts I and II of Appendix A - first buzzing on the mouthpiece *and then on the horn*. This could take an hour. At the end of this time, reflexes should be working again. After working through Parts I and II, put the horn away and come back later in the day and try again. Do not continue to practice - especially playing literature. You will only reinforce bad reflexes!

Making Adjustments to Part I for the Morning After Warm Up

The morning after warm up is necessary on days after you abused your embouchure in some way. This may have occurred, for example, during an unusually heavy playing day, a very demanding performance, or any marching band rehearsal. On this type of day you need to spend more time doing mouthpiece buzzing.

Instead of starting with Appendix A, Part I Mouthpiece Buzzing exercises, begin with *mouthpiece buzzing* on the Long Tone exercise in Part II. This will isolate the four reflexes without adding the lip contraction to produce the whole-step-slurred interval. Concentrate on the mouthpiece placement, getting a nice open buzz, and even airflow.

Making Adjustments to Part I for the Morning Before Warm Up

The Morning Before Warm Up is used on the day you have a performance. The rules that apply to the Normal Warm Up apply here. If it is a Normal Warm Up day, do a complete warm up of 25-35 minutes several hours before the performance. I consider the warm up to last the entire day, so if you do a complete warm up several hours before the performance, you will be completely refreshed by performance time. You can achieve this even if you had to do some reflex-building as part of the day's warm up. *Never do the Short Warm up on performance day!*

Making Adjustments to Part I for the Short Warm Up

I realize that there are times when a 25-35 minute warm up is not possible. On these days you should still play Parts I, II, III, and IV of Appendix A, but you may cut the warm up time in half by skipping every other musical example. Rather than moving up or down the exercises using half-step intervals, instead use the whole-step intervals. There is only one thing I feel strongly about regarding the Short Warm Up - never do the Short Warm Up two days in a row!

Part II – Long Tones

Normal Warm Up

If you are warming up on a normal day, you have completed the buzzing section in Part I, and are ready to begin the long tone section. At this point you should feel that your warm up is progressing well, and that your **embouchure** is ready to place the mouthpiece in the horn.

In Appendix A, Part II, the Long Tones section, we are adding three reflexes to the four reflexes we concentrated on in Part I.

Air Intake - Take a 1 second breath just as you did with the mouthpiece alone.
Embouchure - Continue to grip the embouchure as the **air intake** begins, just as you did with the mouthpiece alone.
Tongue Strike - Tongue Strike occurs when maximum air has been inhaled with the tongue lightly touching the upper lip through the teeth.
Air Column – After the **tongue strike**, blow the air through the trumpet with the same velocity used with the mouthpiece alone.
Body Carriage - Although we should always think about correct body position, I have chosen to concentrate on it as part of the Long Tone section since we now have the horn in our hands for the first time. Remember, we should think of keywords to help remind us about the correct **body carriage**:

- right hand - tennis ball
- left hand - horn hanging
- erect torso - upper body over the hips
- hands, upper arms, elbows - form an equilateral triangle

Tongue Height - We are now concerned with the placement of the tongue after the **tongue strike** occurs. As stated earlier, the vowel formed inside the mouth will help control the speed of the air passing through it. Remember: faster air = higher pitch. For ease of explanation, I will divide the entire trumpet range into four smaller registers. These registers will vary slightly with individual players, so you should use them as a guide.

Low Register - low F# to D just below the treble clef staff
Middle Register - first line Eb to third line Bb
Upper Register - third line B to G just above the treble clef staff
Extreme Upper Register – Ab one ledger line above the treble clef staff, to the upper note playable by any individual

For the **Low Register** you should use the **tongue strike** vowel "thow". This vowel will drop the tongue into the lowest position possible in the mouth which will allow the air to move through the mouth at the slowest speed.

For the **Middle Register** you should use the **tongue strike** vowel "thah". This vowel will allow the tongue to lay flat in the mouth causing the air to move faster through the mouth than the **tongue strike** vowel "thow".

For the **Upper Register** you should use the **tongue strike** vowel "thih". This vowel will allow the air to move faster still.

For the **Extreme Upper Register** you should use the **tongue strike** vowel "thee". As you progress above high C, two ledger lines above the treble clef staff, the tongue will slide forward in the mouth allowing a small trench in the tongue. When done off the horn/mouthpiece it sounds like "shhhhhhhhh".

An important point must be made here which will clarify the relationship between buzz pitch and the speed of air created by **tongue height.** The buzz pitch is controlled by the contraction of the lips, which determines how big or open the resultant tone quality will be - not what specific pitch will sound. Since we are not concerned with pitch at this point, we do the mouthpiece buzzing prior to placing the mouthpiece into the horn. The **tongue height**, on the other hand, controls the speed of the air through the buzz that will result in a specific pitch.

Anchor - As you remember, **anchor** is the place on the **embouchure** where the weight of the horn is placed. I assign the **anchor** placement according to the four registers listed above. As in register definition, individual applications may vary.

For the **Low Register** use an **anchor** placement more on the upper lip than the lower lip. Even though the lower lip vibrates sympathetically, this placement will allow the lower lip the freedom to vibrate more than in the other registers. This produces a bigger sound in the low register. Putting the weight of the horn on the upper lip will not cause an endurance problem in the low register.

For the **Middle Register** use an **anchor** which is more on the lower lip. The upper lip needs to vibrate more than the lower to produce a bigger sound in the middle register.

For the **Upper and Extreme Upper** registers, the **anchor** should be on the lower lip. The upper lip must do almost all of the vibrating for the upper and extreme upper registers. Lack of endurance in trumpet playing can be traced directly to too much horn weight on the upper lip in the upper registers.

As you work through the Long Tones section exercises, try to allow the first four reflexes to fire on their own without your conscious thought. Concentrate instead on the three new reflexes:

> **Body Position**
> **Tongue Height**
> **Anchor**

You should see significant progress in approximately three weeks.

Making Adjustments to Part II for the Morning After Warm Up

If you had a heavy playing day yesterday, you will need to start buzzing on the mouthpiece in the Long Tones section. Concentrate on the first four reflexes:

> **Air Intake**
> **Embouchure**
> **Tongue Strike**
> **Air Column**

- Take a one second breath.
- Grip the **embouchure** during **air intake.**
- **Tongue strike** should occur when maximum air has been inhaled, allowing the tongue to lightly touch the upper lip through the teeth.
- Hold each note until you run out of air.
- Pull the mouthpiece off the **embouchure** after each note.
- Rest as long as it took you to play each note.
- Continue to ascend until you feel your throat closing.
- Go back to Part I and begin the Mouthpiece Buzzing exercises adding the eighth note slurs. The lip slurs are done by contracting the lips.

Making Adjustments to Part II for the Morning Before Warm Up

There are no adjustments required in Part II, Long Tones, for a Morning Before Warm Up.

Making Adjustments to Part II for the Short Warm Up

The adjustments required for Part II, Long Tones, for a Short Warm Up are similar to those made for the Part I, Mouthpiece Buzzing. You should play every other musical example in an effort to save time.

Part III - Descending Slurred Arpeggios

Part III of your daily warm up is the same whether you are doing a normal, morning before, or a morning after warm up. This distinguishes it from Part's I and II. The Short Warm Up still requires an adjustment which is the same as Part I and Part II - merely skip every other musical example due to time constraints. Appendix A, Part III, Descending Slurred Arpeggios, will involve adding another level to the **tongue height** reflex, and add the last reflex called:

Pivot - You will recall that the term **anchor** is the location of the weight of the horn on the embouchure and the **pivot** is defined by the movement of the **anchor** from the bottom lip to the top lip when playing in the low ranges.

This exercise also requires you to slur into the range below the natural horn called the pedal range. The reasons for practicing in the pedal range are surrounded by myths. Let's talk about what pedal practice will do for you.

Practice in extreme ranges, high or low, will strengthen the playable range of the instrument. This exercise takes you into the extreme low register and it's primary goal is to strengthen the low register of the instrument. This strengthening applies to tone quality, power and flexibility. You will notice that I have changed the fingerings of the pedal tones. I have done this in order to make them easier to play. Since you will rarely, if ever, be called upon to play them in a performance, I believe that in this case, easier is better. Another factor that makes them easier is that the last note on the natural horn and the first pedal note are now fingered the same. This will allow you to slur to the pedal note with greater ease. Note: 1-2-3+ indicates all three valves plus the third valve slide extended.

- As you work through the descending slur exercises, try to allow the first seven reflexes to fire on their own without your conscious thought. Concentrate instead on the **pivot** reflex listed above. You should see significant progress in approximately three weeks.

- As you can see, the exercise starts on third space C and continues with a descending slurred major arpeggio. Progress through the Sound Production Cycle as before with the following change: place your tongue at the height you need for the first pitch required, "thih" for third space C, and move the tongue down as you move the weight of the horn from the bottom lip to the top lip as you descend. This means that the tongue and the horn will move simultaneously in opposite directions.

- The metronome marking indicated is half note = 44. This exercise is to be played slowly. Do not hurry.

- As you descend, try to open your teeth slightly. This will roll your lips inward inside the mouthpiece cup, slowing the air stream slightly. This will drop the buzz pitch and open the width of each note's tone quality. Since your jaw is hinged, when you open your teeth your lower jaw will come in slightly. To compensate for this, move the lower jaw outward as you open your teeth.

- When you reach the fermata, treat this note as a long tone just as you did in the previous exercise.

- At the rest, you must rest as long as it took you to play each descending slurred arpeggio.

- Pull the horn off the **embouchure** and start the Sound Production Cycle over for each arpeggio.

- Try to go lower each day until you can play the entire exercise.

- If you want to experiment, continue below pedal C, using the same fingerings you did for the octave above.

- Work toward the widest tone possible on each pedal note. Remember - wide tone is controlled by low buzz pitch.

Part IV - Ascending Tongued Arpeggios

Normal Warm Up

You are now ready to complete your daily warm up by adding four **tongue strikes** in a row, and moving **tongue height** and **pivot** for use in the upper and extreme upper registers. These exercises are located in Appendix A, Part IV, Ascending Tongued Arpeggios.

This exercise requires you to practice four **tongue strikes** as you play an ascending major arpeggio. As you ascend, you must **pivot** and move the **anchor** from it's position for the first note in the arpeggio to the position needed for the last note in the arpeggio. You must also move the **tongue height** to it's position to achieve the correct air speed for each note in the arpeggio.

- As you work through the Ascending Tongued exercises, try to allow all reflexes to fire without conscious thought.
- The exercises start on low F#, and continue through high C above the treble clef staff. Progress through the Sound Production Cycle as before, placing your tongue at the required height needed for the first pitch in each arpeggio. **Pivot** the **anchor** and raise the **tongue height** as you ascend.
- Note the metronomic marking is set for you to play this exercise slightly faster than the descending slurs.
- To help the upper note respond, try adding a small crescendo as you move from the third note to the last.
- When you reach the fermata, treat this as a long tone, the same way you did in the previous exercise.
- At the rest you must rest as long as it took you to play each ascending arpeggio.
- Pull the horn off the **embouchure** and start the Sound Production Cycle over for each arpeggio.
- Try to go higher each day until you can play the high C. If you cannot reach the high C, make three attempts at the highest note you can play, then quit. *Three strikes and you're out!* When you reach the high C, do not go higher at this time.

Remember that you are warming up. Extreme high register building is not done during the warm up.

Making Adjustments to Part IV for the Morning After Warm Up

There are no adjustments necessary.

Making Adjustments to Part IV for the Morning Before Warm Up

You should play every other musical example.

Making Adjustments to Part IV for the Short Warm Up

You should play every other musical example.

Single Tonguing Exercises

The basic idea of single tonguing is to interrupt the **air column** with the tongue, not to stop it. The single tonguing exercises will take you through a step-by-step progression which will enable you to learn the proper reflexes necessary to single tongue with speed and clarity.

You are practicing the reflexes related to single tonguing each day during your warm up on the mouthpiece and the horn during buzzing and long tone exercises. This section of the book is intended to give you more detail at the beginning of your learning, and provide you with some direction on a day when you are having difficulty with tonguing.

Begin by taking out the Long Tones exercise, Part II from Appendix A. To review, the buzz will start without help from the tongue in any way if the air speed is fast enough. We cannot wait for the air speed to build up, so we tongue. Let's discover where the buzz starts for you.

- Begin by looking at the middle C. Start blowing air into the horn without tonguing until the air is fast enough to make the middle C sound.
- Experiment with this feeling until you know exactly when the note will begin. Now blow enough air to get the note started *while lightly touching your upper lip between your teeth.*
- You will notice that the note starts immediately with an attack that is clean, clear and without a hard beginning!
- Continue through the Long Tone exercise in a similar manner remembering to use the **pivot** and changing the **tongue height** to achieve notes in the various registers.

After you have worked on one **tongue strike** during long tones, you should start the Single Tonguing exercise in Appendix B, with three **tongue strikes**.

- You will start in the middle register that will require an **anchor** set-up that is mostly on the bottom lip.
- You will move toward the upper and lower registers in step-wise increments.
- Concentrate on connecting each note to the next and interrupting the **air column** with the tongue. Remember, allow the tongue to lightly touch the upper lip through the teeth to restart the buzz.
- Progress through the exercises adding **tongue strikes.** Do not allow the throat to close while performing these exercises.

Double Tonguing Exercises

There is some debate among trumpet teachers about which multiple tonguing pattern, double or triple, should be learned first. It is my opinion that it is easier to begin with double tonguing.

The technique involved with double tonguing is very similar to the single tonguing technique in that the initial **tongue strike** is the same, e.g. "thih". The "double" comes from the fact that the second note's articulation comes from the tongue interrupting the air flow by making contact with the roof of the mouth by using the consonant "K" sound i.e. "kih". The vowel formed by the cavity of the mouth remains the same as it was when the single **tongue strike** occurred. The idea here is that this "double" method will be faster than the single **tongue strike** alone.

I like to make a very important distinction here. When articulating any multiple tongue, double or triple, the entire tongue needs to be focused as far forward in the mouth as possible. This is consistent no matter where the tongue is usually placed for the single **tongue strike**. That's why, in the example above, I used the vowel shape "thih". I would try to use "thih" as far down in the range as possible. As you proceed upward, try to get to "thee" as soon as possible.

This is the goal: "thee-kee"," thee-kee", "thee-kee"! The tongue should be focused as far forward as possible so that the distance *between* the strike of the "th" and the strike of the "K" is as small as possible. This closeness will enable much greater speed than the "Tu-Ku" vowel/consonant formation.

Proceed with the Double Tonguing exercises, Appendix B, in the following manner:

- Using the "Th" **tongue strike** as you have been for the single tonguing exercises, begin the double tonguing exercises with the a.) articulation.
- Try to make the resultant attack of the "th" match the "K" sound exactly. You will probably find that you can "K" tongue harder than you thought you would be able to.
- After you are able to match the two sounds on the notes/rhythms outlined in the first exercise, try the b.) articulation on the same exercise.
- Do not go on to the two eighth note/quarter note pattern until you have accomplished the first pattern for the two octave span.
- Remember, building reflexes takes concentrated practice over time. Be patient and the results will come.
- Master each pattern before proceeding to the next. Master the a.) pattern before attempting the b.) pattern.

Triple Tonguing Exercises

As you may have assumed by now, the process used for triple tonguing is very similar to that used for double tonguing. The obvious difference is the fact that two "th" consonants are used before the "K" consonant is used. The fact that you have concentrated so long on moving the "K" **tongue strike** as far forward as possible will make the triple pattern relatively easy to master.

There is, however, no shortcut for learning to triple tongue. Slow concentrated practice on the a.), then b.) patterns, will be the only way to learn the triple tonguing technique.

- Using the "Th" **tongue strike** as you have been for the single and double tonguing exercises, begin the Triple Tonguing exercises from Appendix B, with the a.) articulation.
- Try to make the resultant attack of the two "th" **tongue strikes** match the "K" sound exactly. Again, you will probably feel that you can "K" tongue even harder than you did in the double tonguing exercises.
- After you are able to match the three sounds on the notes/rhythms outlined in the first exercise, try the b.) articulation on the same exercise.
- Do not go on to the three eighth note/dotted quarter note pattern until you have accomplished the first pattern for the two octave span.
- Remember, building reflexes takes concentrated practice over time. Be patient and the results will come.
- Master each pattern before proceeding to the next! Master the a.) pattern before attempting the b.) pattern.

UNIT 17   ASCENDING SLURRED INTERVALS

Ascending Slurred Intervals

One of the most difficult trumpet techniques to master is the ascending slur. This technique becomes more difficult as the interval increases. The exercises in Appendix C, Ascending Slurred Interval Exercises, should be used in two different ways:

1. As an exercise to learn ascending slurring by interval
2. As an exercise to practice for endurance

The technique needed for playing the ascending slur is related to all of the other techniques we have studied so far. To review, pitch is related to air speed. If we want a low note to sound, we need slower air. If we want a high note to sound, we need faster air. The problem with the ascending slur is that we do not have the luxury of a tongue strike for the second or slurred note, and must achieve faster air some other way. In this case, we'll rely on *raising the tongue inside the mouth.* If, for example, we wanted to slur from middle C to second line G, we would place our tongue at the proper height for playing the middle C, "thah", then as we play the C we move the tongue to the position for G, "theh". When the tongue moves up, the space in the mouth becomes smaller, and the air moves faster. Be careful not to close your throat to achieve this effect. When the air speed reaches that which is necessary for the G, it will sound. If you have trouble in the beginning, you probably need to move your tongue *farther faster.* You will find that the descending slur is much easier to learn.

- Master each like-fingered slur interval by note value, before continuing to the faster slurs. For example, practice all the intervals using half notes before progressing to quarter notes.

- Keep the throat open as you ascend and allow the faster air to do the work. Pull the trumpet off the embouchure and rest after each slurred figure.

UNIT 18 THE UPPER REGISTER

Work in the upper register actually has its' beginnings in Appendix A, Daily Warm Up Exercises, Part IV. To review, during this exercise you played an ascending arpeggio using four **tongue strikes**. You ended this part of the warm up at high C, two ledger lines above the treble clef staff. Or, you had not reached the high C yet, and you ended when you reached the "three strike" limit.

If you have not reached the high C yet, you should go back to Appendix A, Daily Warm Up Exercises, Part IV and practice it until you have achieved the high C before proceeding with the exercises in this unit. Once you have done this, you may start the exercises in Appendix D, Upper Register Exercises.

These exercises should be done at the beginning of the second practice session of the day. Do not sacrifice literature practice to practice the upper register. Keep the following points in mind during the practice session:

- As you ascend, be sure to use the **pivot** in combination with the upward movement of the tongue.
- The higher the note you are attempting, the more the tongue should be focused forward. Think of telling someone to be quiet - "shhhhhh".
- Pull the trumpet off the **embouchure** after each ascending arpeggio.
- Remember, "three strikes and you're out."
- Upper register practice should not be attempted when you are physically tired.
- Upper register practice sessions should be separated by at least one day.
- After you feel comfortable with the Upper Register Exercise I in Appendix D, you may proceed to the Upper Register Exercise II.

- You will notice that Exercise II asks you to add a slurred half step at the end of each ascending arpeggio. You will quickly realize that the difference in effort for the additional half step is very small.

- When slurring to the half step, keep the air moving and move the tongue forward in the mouth as you raise it slightly. You may even add a small crescendo at the point of the slur.

- Try to extend your range further each week.

- Expansion of your range will come in small increments of half steps. Do not get frustrated with slow progress in this area. As you understand what your body needs to do, progress will occur.

UNIT 19 PRACTICING FOR ENDURANCE

Building endurance is affected by mouthpiece selection, so let's discuss that area first.

As you remember from Unit 14, Buying a Trumpet and Mouthpiece, players who play for long periods each day should use mouthpieces with larger rings. I believe that the 1C mouthpiece should be used by trumpet players who play four or five hours per day. If trumpet players try to play with a large mouthpiece without the discipline of playing at least four or five hours per day, endurance will definitely be a problem. It takes a great deal of strength to play on the big mouthpiece rings because more of each lip is inside the mouthpiece cup and it takes more strength to keep that much flesh firm during the grip. If you are fairly certain that you are playing on the correct size cup and rim combination for the amount of playing you do each day, you will be able to benefit from endurance practice.

Endurance is achieved by building strength in the facial muscles. This begins by practicing all of the ascending slurred intervals in one sitting until you are completely fatigued. Until now, you have only practiced slurs individually or as part of **pivot** and **anchor** practice. The goal of endurance practice is to increase the amount of time you can play before the **embouchure** collapses.

Use the musical exercises from Appendix C, Ascending Slurred Interval Exercises, in the following manner:

- Start with the interval of the third, using the half-note rhythm. Play the entire exercise without relaxing the facial muscles or stopping after each slur to rest.
- If you can play through the entire half-note section, proceed to the next rhythm in thirds, progressing until your facial muscles fatigue, *then rest*.

- Do not press the horn up on the **embouchure**. Let the facial muscles do the work.
- If you cannot play through the entire half-note section, stop and rest when your facial muscles are fatigued. When you are able, continue from the point *where you stopped*.
- Progress through all of the rhythms for the interval of the third, resting when fatigued, and then move on to the interval of the fourth. Progress through all of the rhythms.
- Continue in the same manner through all of the interval exercises.

If you can play through all of the slurred interval exercises in all of the rhythms as outlined above, without the facial muscles collapsing, you may then continue with the musical exercises in Appendix E, Endurance Exercises.

When do I get to stop?

As your facial muscles fatigue, the time that you are able to play before the muscles collapse will become shorter, and the rest period will become longer. The rest period could be as long as 3 or 4 minutes toward the end of the endurance practice session. You stop when the facial muscles will not grip to form the **embouchure**.

Notes:

Endurance practice should not be done more than twice a week.

You should do the Morning After Warm Up the day after endurance practice is done.

Do not attempt an endurance practice session within five days prior to a performance.

Earlier in the book, you talked about tapering before a performance. Is the taper a part of endurance practice?

Yes. Athletes of all kinds have known about and used the "taper" technique when approaching the big game, meet, or athletic contest. The philosophy is based upon the idea that muscle strength will actually increase if the amount of use is increased for a period of time and then tapered, or gradually shortened, in the last few days before a competition.

The endurance problem most trumpet players face is directly attributable to the fact that their practice habits are so poor that they are forced to do too much of their practicing in the last few days prior to a performance. There is just no time to taper. In order to use the technique of tapering, one must be organized throughout the entire practice routine.

Each player reacts differently to endurance practice. For example, I rarely do more than one endurance practice session per week, and I only do them two to six weeks before a demanding performance. Most of the time one session a week will be adequate. Most players find that they can increase playing time with each endurance practice session before the **embouchure** collapses. That should always be the goal.

After you have established an endurance building routine, you will be able to feel when your endurance needs to be built for a particular concert or solo performance. If endurance is properly built in the weeks prior to a performance and the music to be performed is properly learned, you can taper the amount of playing you do each day, culminating with a complete warm up the day of the performance. I would avoid doing any endurance practice closer than five days prior to a performance. This will allow you sufficient time to taper. There should be no need to practice literature on performance day. It's too late by then.

Which kind of vibrato is the best to learn?

Vibrato is the bending of pitch created by movement of either the hand or the jaw. Hand vibrato pulls the mouthpiece away from the **embouchure**, causing the pitch to drop. Jaw vibrato is much more commonly used and involves a combination of relaxing the **embouchure**, opening the teeth, and lowering the tongue. Jaw vibrato is the type I choose to use and teach. To produce a jaw vibrato, use the syllable "yaw" to lower the pitch, and "eee" to raise it. By alternating these syllables, "yaw-eee-yaw-eee-yaw-eee-yaw", a vibrato is produced.

We have already discussed the effect of opening the sound by opening the teeth slightly, thus creating a lower buzz pitch. It is more difficult, and less desirable, to lip a note even a small amount upward in pitch, since the result would tend to produce a pinched sound. We also know that it is undesirable to open the teeth too far. The "yaw" syllable used for vibrato is opening the teeth enough to lower the pitch without losing control. The vibrato technique is easily done on a trumpet.

When we play a straight tone, we create a *tone center*. The tone center is the pitch produced by the trumpet player blowing straight through the tone, without the application of vibrato. Vibrato will lower the tone center creating a *median intonation center*. This is the median between the highest and lowest points of pitch fluctuation and is lower than the tone center. The trumpet will need to be tuned slightly sharp in situations where you will primarily be playing with a vibrato in order to compensate for this.

The following graphic shows the tone center (1.), the shape of the vibrato (2.), and the resultant median intonation center (3.).

1. _____ 2. 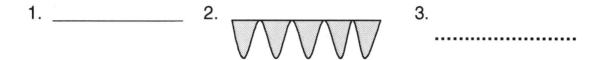 3. ....

When these three elements are overlapped, as shown below, they demonstrate graphically the effect that vibrato has upon intonation.

The goal of vibrato practice is to have complete control over the width and the speed of the pitch variation. To practice the vibrato, you will use the musical examples from Appendix A, Part II, Long Tones. While playing the long tones indicated, apply the rhythms from Appendix F, Vibrato Exercises.

- The shape of the vibrato should resemble a smooth sine wave, as shown in the above graphic.
- Speed should be somewhere between the triplet and the sixteenth note value, approximately 5 vibrations per second.
- Start each long tone on it's tone center, then open the teeth slightly, using the "yaw" sound until the pitch lowers, then close the teeth, using the "eee", to the position where you started at the tone center.
- Go through all of the long tones using this "yaw-eee-yaw-eee" system. Use the rhythms indicated in Appendix F, Vibrato Exercises.

- Once the warm up routine is firmly established and you are sure that you are playing with an open sound, you may practice vibrato during the long tone section of the warm up, effectively warming up and practicing vibrato at the same time.
- You should expect to develop a consistent vibrato within three to four months.

Appendix A
Daily Warm Up Exercises
Part I - Mouthpiece Buzzing

Reflex:
* Air Intake
* Embouchure
* Tongue Strike
* Air Column

Quarter Note = 66

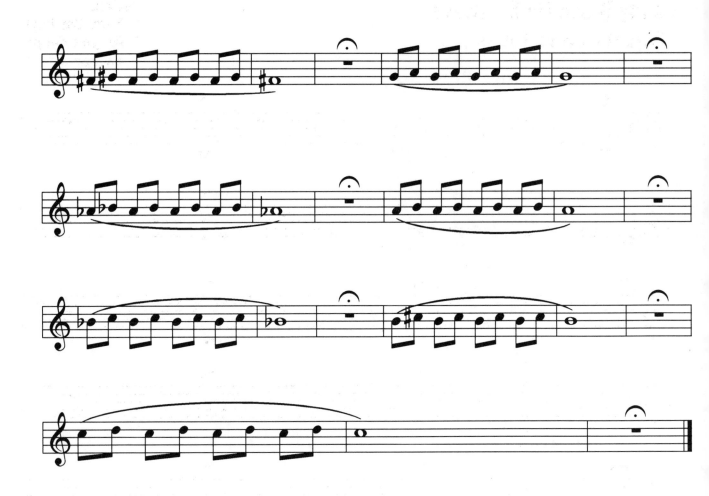

Daily Warm Up Exercises
Part II - Long Tones

Daily Warm Up Exercises
Part III - Descending Slurred Arpeggios

Half Note = 62

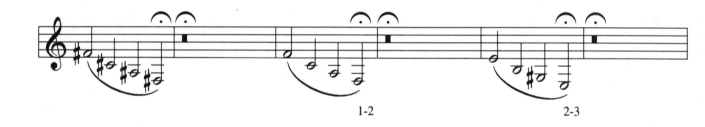

1-2   2-3

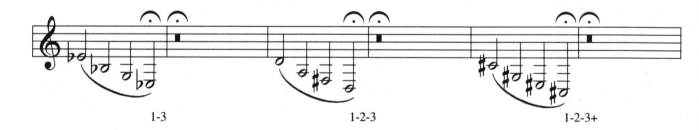

1-3   1-2-3   1-2-3+

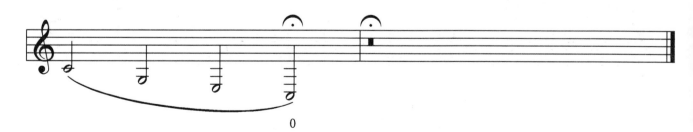

0

Daily Warm Up Exercises
Part IV - Ascending Tongued Arpeggios

Reflex:
* Tongue Strike
* Tongue Height

Half Note = 72

79

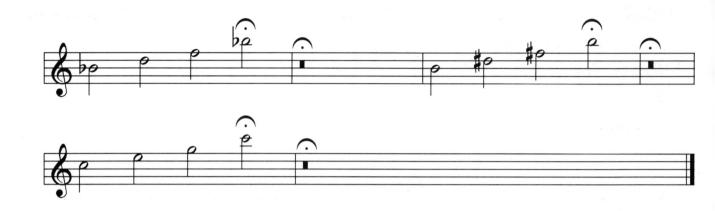

Appendix B
Tonguing Exercises
Single Tonguing

Quarter Note = 96-116

81

Apply the following rhythms (Tongue Strikes) to the previous notes.

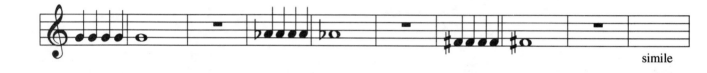

simile

simile

simile

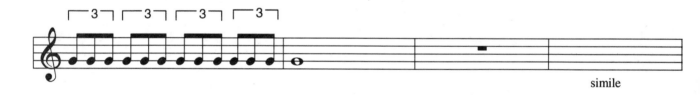

simile

Tonguing Exercises
Double Tonguing

Quarter Note = 96-200

a.) Th Th Th   K K K   simile
b.) Th K Th   Th K Th   simile

83

Apply the a.) articulation to the following examples using the previous notes.
Apply the b.) articulation to the following examples using the previous notes.

a.) Th   Th   Th   K   K   K   simile
b. Th   K   Th   Th   K   Th   simile

a.) Th Th Th   K K K   Th Th Th   K K K   simile
b.) Th K Th   Th K Th   Th K Th   Th K Th   simile

a.) Th Th Th Th   K K K K   Th Th Th Th   K K K K   simile
b.) Th K Th K   Th K Th K   Th K Th K   Th K Th K   simile

a.) Th Th Th Th K K K K   Th Th Th Th K K K K   Th Th Th Th K K K K   Th Th Th Th K K K K   simile
b.) Th K Th K Th K Th K   Th K Th K Th K Th K   Th K Th K Th K Th K   Th K Th K Th K Th K   Th K Th K   simile

84

Tonguing Exercises
Triple Tonguing

Reflex:
* Tongue Strike

Quarter Note = 96-200

Apply the a.) articulation to the following examples using the previous notes.
Apply the b.) articulation to the following examples using the previous notes.

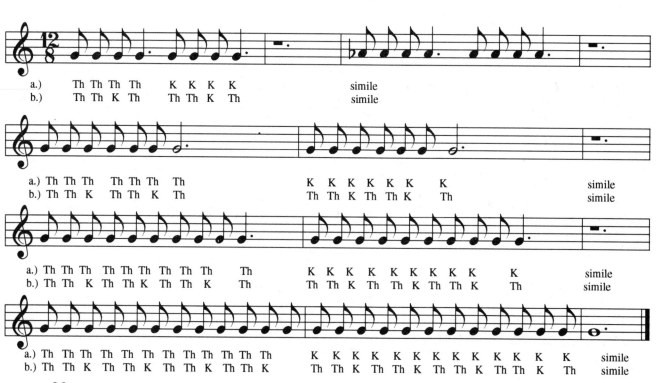

a.)   Th Th Th Th   K K K K   simile
b.)   Th Th K Th   Th Th K Th   simile

a.) Th Th Th Th Th Th Th   K K K K K K K   simile
b.) Th Th K Th Th K Th   Th Th K Th Th K Th   simile

a.) Th Th Th Th Th Th Th Th Th   Th   K K K K K K K K K   simile
b.) Th Th K Th Th K Th Th K   Th   Th Th K Th Th K Th Th K   Th   simile

a.) Th Th Th Th Th Th Th Th Th Th Th Th Th   K K K K K K K K K K K K K   simile
b.) Th Th K Th Th K Th Th K Th Th K   Th Th K Th Th K Th Th K Th Th K Th   simile

86

Appendix C
Ascending Slurred Interval Exercises
Intervals of the Third

Reflex:
* Tongue Height
* Anchor
* Pivot

Quarter Note = 96

1-3   2-3

1-2   1

2   0

1-2   1

2   0

0   2

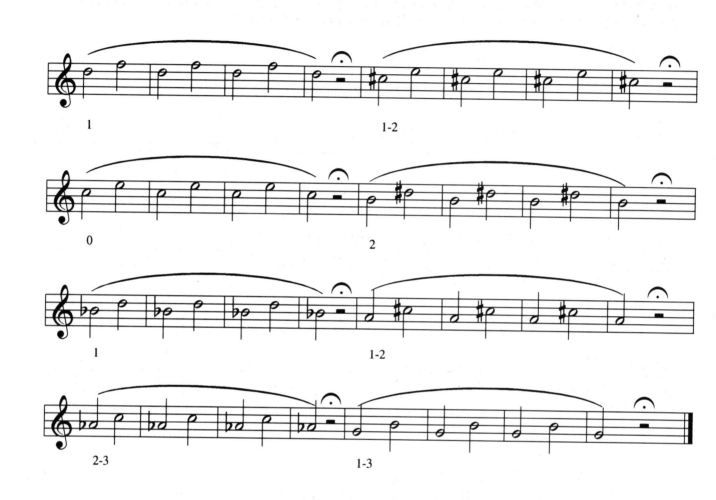

1

1-2

0

2

1

1-2

2-3

1-3

**Play the slurred exercises from the previous pages using the rhythm patterns below.
Do not start these patterns until the half-note slurs are mastered.**

Ascending Slurred Interval Exercises
Intervals of the Fourth

Reflex:
* Tongue Height
* Anchor
* Pivot

Quarter Note = 96

**Play the slurred exercises from the previous page using the rhythm patterns below.
Do not start these patterns until the half-note slurs are mastered.**

Ascending Slurred Interval Exercises
Intervals of the Fifth

Reflex:
* Tongue Height
* Anchor
* Pivot

Quarter Note = 88

92

Play the slurred exercises from the previous page using the rhythm patterns below. Do not start these patterns until the half-note slurs are mastered.

Ascending Slurred Interval Exercises
Intervals of the Octave

Reflex:
* Tongue Height
* Anchor
* Pivot

Quarter Note = 96

Play the slurred exercises from the previous page using the rhythm patterns below.
Do not start these patterns until the half-note slurs are mastered.

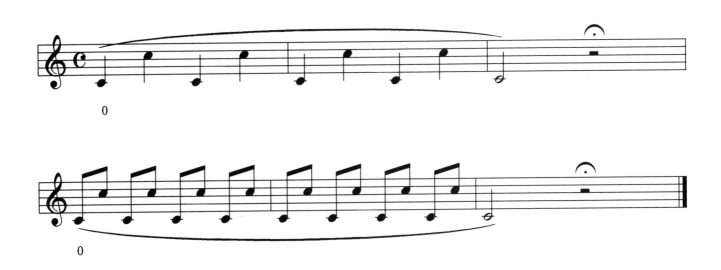

Ascending Slurred Interval Exercises
Intervals of the Tenth

Reflex:
* Tongue Height
* Anchor
* Pivot

Quarter Note = 96

Play the slurred exercises from the previous page using the rhythm patterns below. Do not start these patterns until the half-note slurs are mastered.

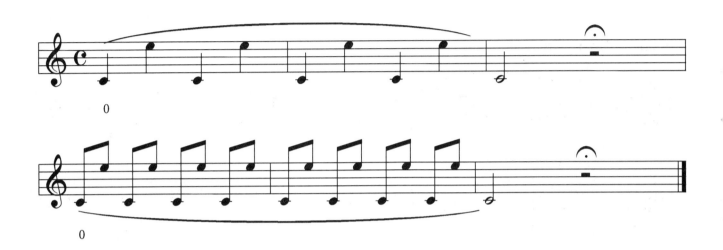

Appendix D
Upper Register Exercises
Exercise I

Quarter Note = 96

Upper Register Exercises
Exercise II

Quarter Note = 96

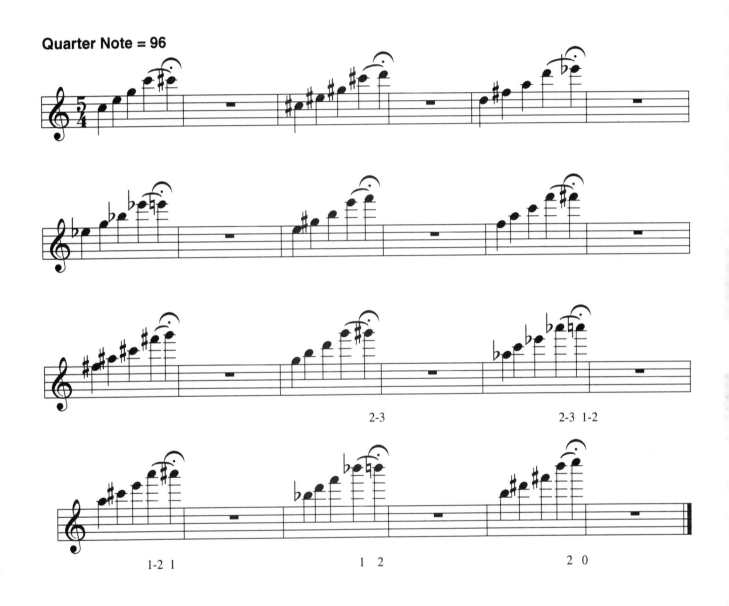

Appendix E
Endurance Exercises

This endurance practice section may be started only after completing the Ascending Slurred Interval Exercises in Appendix C.

Quarter Note = 96

Play the endurance exercises from the previous page using the rhythm patterns below. Remember to rest when fatigued, then continue from where you stopped.

1-3

simile

1-3

simile

Appendix F
Vibrato Exercises

Apply each rhythm from the following exercises to Long Tones, Part II from the Daily Warm Up Exercises, Appendix A. Blow slightly sharper on each note marked with a plus sign (+). Do this by closing your teeth slightly.

Quarter Note = 60-64

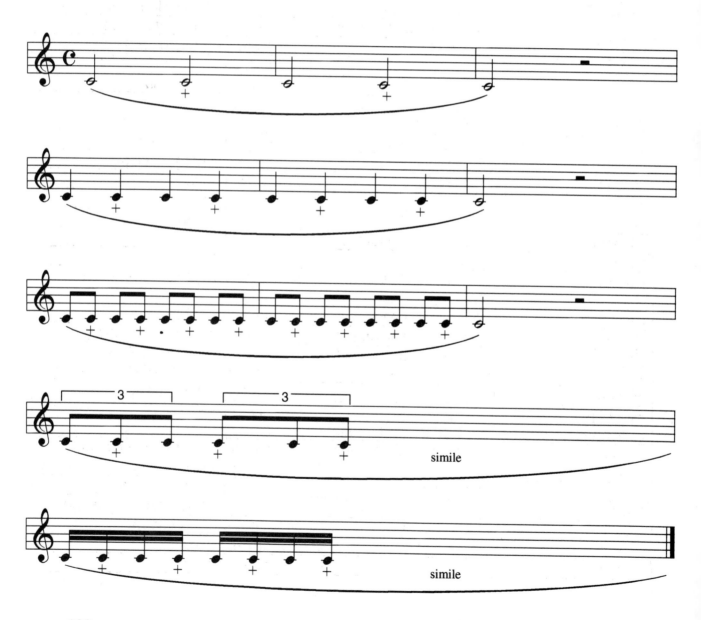

APPENDIX G   RECOMMENDED LITERATURE LIST

Composer	Title	Demands
Alary	Morceau de Concours	taxing, range, fast single tongue
Anonymous (arr. by Kehrhahn)	Thema and Variations	Eb cornet, technically difficult
Artunian	Concerto	difficult, double-tonguing, single-tonguing
Balay	Petite Piece Concertante	key, fast single tongue
Balay	Prelude et Ballade	Prelude is difficult, separate mvts.
Barat	Andante and Scherzo	very difficult, recital piece
Bellini	Concerto	range, technique, endurance
Bellstedt	Napoli	technique
Brandt	Concertpiece No. 1	moderately difficult
Charlie	Solo de Concours	difficult
Clark	Shores…Mighty Pacific	very technical, single tongue
Clark	The Carnival of Venice	very technical, difficult
Corelli	Sonata VIII	four movements - all good
Dubois	Choral	lots of endurance
Enesco	Legend	in 6, technical
Forestier	Fantasie Brillante	technically difficult
Giannini	Concerto for Trumpet	very difficult, range
Goedicke	Concert Etude	double tonguing
Handel	Sonata for Trumpet	moderatally technical, moderate endurance
Handel	Adagio and Allegro	moderate range
Handel	Concerto for Trumpet	endurance, technical, taxing
Haydn	Concerto for Trumpet	a standard in trumpet literature; considered a "must do"
Hindemith	Sonate	difficult in many areas
Honegger	Intrada	moderately difficult
Hovhaness	Prayer of Saint Gregory	good recital piece
Hummel	Concerto for Trumpet	a standard in trumpet literature; considered a "must do"
Ibert	Impromptu	C trumpet, recital piece
Kennan	Sonata	rhythm, compound time, range
Mozart	Concerto in D	high range, C trumpet
Mozart	Larghetto	range, recital piece
Peeters	Sonata	single tongue

Persichetti	Hollow Men	range, control
Purcell	Sonata No. 1	single tongue, intonation
Richter	Sonata from the Seranade	C trumpet with Organ, easy
Riisager	Concertino	difficult
Ropartz	Andante et Allegro	endurance, single tongue
Sachse	Concertino	range, technique, for Bb, Bb piccolo, or Eb trumpet
Tartini	Concerto in C	very difficult, piccolo trumpet
Tomasi	Concerto for Trumpet in C	very difficult, C trumpet
Turrin	Psalm from Two Portraits	difficult, flugelhorn
Turrin	Escapade	for piccolo trumpet, very difficult
Wal-Berg	Concerto for Trumpet	single tonguing, flexibility

Share the Physical Approach with Others!

Do you know a trumpet student or teacher who could benefit from the unique ideas presented in <u>A Physical Approach to Playing the Trumpet</u>? Spread the word!

Additional copies of <u>A Physical Approach to Playing the Trumpet</u> are available in bookstores or directly from the publisher! To order, simply send $16.95 per book (Michigan residents add 6% sales tax) plus $3.50 postage and handling for one book, $1.50 for each additional book, to:

WaveSong Press
1138 Fairfield Dr.
Hudsonville, MI   49426

Include your mailing address and phone number along with your check or money order. Make your check payable to "WaveSong Press". Quantity discounts are available. Contact us for details. Visit our website to order using a major credit card.

Phone: (616) 457-0562
E-mail: wavesong@worldnet.att.net
Website: www.trumpetbook.com